D0060281

ALSO BY CHARLES R. MORRIS

*The Cost of Good Intentions: New York City and the Liberal Experiment, 1960–1975*

*A Time of Passion: America, 1960–1980*

*Iron Destinies, Lost Opportunities: The Postwar Arms Race*

*The Coming Global Boom*

*Computer Wars*
(with Charles H. Ferguson)

# The AARP

# The AARP

## *America's Most Powerful Lobby and the Clash of Generations*

Charles R. Morris

RANDOM HOUSE

 Published in the United States by Times Books, a division of Random House, Inc., New York, and simultaneously in Canada by Random House of Canada Limited, Toronto.

Library of Congress Cataloging-in-Publication Data
Morris, Charles R.
The AARP: America's most powerful lobby and the clash of generations / Charles R. Morris.
p. cm.
Includes bibliographical references and index.
ISBN 0-8129-2753-2
1. American Association of Retired Persons—History. 2. Retirees—United States—Social conditions. I. Title.

306.3′8′0973—dc20 95-46878

Printed in the United States of America on acid-free paper

24689753

First Edition

BOOK DESIGN BY JANE FAY

# *Acknowledgments*

I should like especially to thank Harriet Rubinson, a most competent and conscientious research assistant; the very large number of AARP executives, staffers, and volunteers who submitted patiently to my questions and requests for information; Chuck Blahous of Senator Alan Simpson's staff; Ellen Stark of *Money* magazine; and Andy Rooney of CBS News. It is a pleasure to work with Peter Osnos, Steve Wasserman, and Nancy Inglis at Times Books, and with my agent, Tim Seldes. As always, my wife, Beverly, tolerated my disappearance into another book with affection and good humor.

# *Contents*

# *Introduction*

A SENATE HEARING ROOM is designed to be intimidating. The senators sit in large easy chairs arranged in a semicircle behind a beautifully polished dark-wood dais, with the great seal of the Senate behind them. The witness table is about six feet lower than the dais, so the witness peers up as from a well, and senators address their questions downward. The high ceiling makes the room vertical, so witnesses look small, and probably feel that way. A black tangle of electronic gear separates the witness from the row or two of seating reserved for supporters. Double rows of press tables line both sides of the room, and reporters lounge, and joke, and watch dispassionately for a hint of blood or drama.

Senator Alan Simpson's two days of hearings into the finances of the American Association of Retired Persons in June of 1995 were meant to be unfriendly. Simpson is a self-described "skinny old guy" from Wyoming, with a casual style that can't conceal a rapier intelligence and shrewd wit. He is passionately devoted to the cause of balanced federal budgets, and to reining in the cost of Social Security and Medicare. Senior entitlements are the "third rail of American politics," in Tip O'Neill's phrase—"Touch it and you die"—and Simpson is one of only a handful of members of Congress in either party who is willing to make his stand without hiding behind equivocations and double-talk.

The American Association of Retired Persons, or AARP, is the premier lobbyist for elderly causes, an "eight-hundred-pound gorilla" in Washington politics. Some 32 million people over fifty, two thirds of them over sixty-five, belong to AARP. Every month, they receive political bulletins from AARP's Washington headquarters. No other age group is as politically sensitive, or as politically involved, or votes as reliably, as seniors, so it is no wonder that politicians of all parties compete for invitations to AARP legislative conferences, or scheme to have their picture appear in AARP newsletters. It is no accident that for much of the two days of hearings, Simpson is alone at the dais, and when he sits by himself, the room's visual strategy reverses and subtly reinforces his isolation. Two other senators, John Breaux of Louisiana and David Pryor of Arkansas, both conservative Democrats who believe in balanced budgets, make cameo appearances but take pains to be friendly to AARP.

The hearings are nominally about the appropriateness of tax code provisions that permit nonprofit lobbying organizations to receive federal grants or earn business income. A bit awkwardly, it turns out that there are thousands of nonprofits, from fishermen's associations to the National Rifle Association, who are more dependent on grants or outside income than AARP is. In truth, however, the hearings are really an early salvo for coming balanced budget battles, a chance to soften up AARP, expose some chinks in its armor, and give Simpson a platform to rail against "greedy geezers" who are threatening "to impoverish our children and grandchildren" with their incessant demands on the Treasury.

The highlight of the second day is the appearance as a witness of Senator John McCain of Arizona, a handsome, tanned, white-haired man, a war hero with a star-quality glow. McCain mounts a slashing attack on AARP, describing how, in 1989, AARP supported Medicare "Catastrophic Care" provisions that seniors in his state opposed overwhelmingly. AARP was "unrepresentative," he charged, parading as the friend of the aged only to sell them products and win more grants. Simpson thanks him profusely for demonstrating that seniors are the true fiscal conservatives who, in real life, refuse to follow the nostrums peddled by AARP. Indeed, straws in the wind suggest that the politics of senior entitlements is shifting. The audience in the hearing room, mostly young policy types, is remarkably hostile to AARP (a Simpson staffer swears it was not packed). Their body language silently eggs McCain on, and later, when AARP's executive director, Horace Deets, answers questions, there are audible snickers at anything that sounds evasive.

But McCain's testimony underscores the quicksilver character of senior politics. The Medicare bill that AARP supported, and which so infuriated McCain's constituents, required seniors to *pay for* improvements in the program. The wealthiest seniors, who had to pay the most, were the most outraged and threatened to dismantle AARP stone by stone. All senior advocacy organizations supported the bill when it first passed, but all except AARP ran for cover when the protests started. AARP had supported the legislation because it benefited the great majority of seniors, and because the payment requirements were not onerous, and stuck to its guns in the face of the protests. On a fair reading of the history, therefore, it was *McCain* who represented the "greedy geezers" at the Simpson hearings, not AARP. On the legislation in question, in fact, AARP and Simpson had been on the same side.

No public issue looms as large as the coming demographic transformation of America into an elderly nation. American history since World War II is dominated by only a few transforming themes—the creation of the automobile-based economy in the 1950s; the prolonged confrontation with the Soviet Union; coming to terms with a multiracial society. The doubling of the nation's elderly population is the transforming issue that will loom over American politics for the next thirty years. And just as the "youth culture" defined the 1960s, the aged will set the tone for the first half of the twenty-first century, for they are, of course, the same people. But as the baby boomers age, they will become much more dependent and much more expensive to maintain than they ever were as children. As medical science continues to work miracles, their dotage is likely to last a good deal longer than their youth did.

When I began to research the politics of Social Security and Medicare, the public programs that embody the provision America makes for its aged, I decided to begin by concentrating on AARP. I expected to find a primary obstacle to responsible reform, an example of the systemic rigidities blocking change. I was pleasantly surprised to discover that the picture is much more complicated than that. As

Senator McCain's testimony suggests, it is often the loudest voices for fiscal rectitude who really stand up for the "greedy geezers" of the world, while AARP is left with the unhappy task of defending budgetary responsibility. As the following pages will make clear, I found much to criticize in AARP, but on the whole, I believe they are an invaluable policy resource on senior issues, and I expect them to be a critical broker in the process of developing a sustainable, mutually beneficial accommodation to the exigencies of the new demographics. The process of reaching that accommodation will not be easy, it will almost certainly not be polite, and we can't afford to shoot the honest brokers.

The book is divided into three parts. In the first I look closely at AARP, its financial and business activities, its service network, and its powerful lobbying organization. I dredge out some skeletons from old closets, because I think the history is important in its own right, and because it underscores how much the organization has re-created itself in recent years. (I reserve a detailed review of AARP products for an Appendix for interested readers.)

Part II explores the structure and financing of senior entitlement programs, and pinpoints the winners and losers from the current system—yes, Virginia, there are some greedy geezers out there. And I use the recent political history of entitlement reform to demonstrate the fierce emotions that surround these programs.

Part III is devoted to the possibilities of reform, and is a plea for regarding the entitlements issue as a Very Serious Problem but not an Overwhelming

Crisis. I do not think that the continued growth of the health care sector should be cause for alarm; more likely, it will confer important benefits upon the rest of the economy. The section is also a plea for the practice of "muddling through," the true science of politics in America. Sweeping, "comprehensive" reform is just not the way we do things. And happily, I think there are a very large number of practical, piecemeal reforms that will help make the coming transition much easier than it otherwise might be.

# I

# *A Warm and Fuzzy Eight-Hundred-Pound Gorilla*

# Chapter 1

## *The Gorilla at Home*

THE NEW HEADQUARTERS BUILDING of the American Association of Retired Persons on the corner of Sixth and E Streets in Washington's Northwest section is a striking building, a massive riff on classical themes in handsome sand-colored brick and preformed concrete. Ten stories high, and almost a block long, the building is centered on a giant column and arch treatment over a courtyard and promenade and sports a crenellated tower on one end. It is a bold, almost flamboyant design, the kind of strident power-statement that dominates rolling green lawns on corporate campuses.

The front of the building, however, stretches along E Street, a relatively narrow, somewhat down-at-the-heels commercial strip, and it's hard to find a viewing angle to see the design. You have to walk to the corner of Seventh, across the street, and crane back your neck to get even a sharply angled side view of the arch-and-columns and tower. And the building entrance, instead of being under the central arch as one would expect, is displaced to the corner and executed in a distinctly minor key—an unobtrusive ground-level doorway with the organization's name in modest six-inch letters across the top. The door is flanked by storefront windows for pharmacy and information services, and the sandy bricks have a warm, homey feel. Going in and out, you hardly notice the huge structure above.

The sudden shifts of scale are central to an understanding of the Association, or AARP as it is usually called—popped out in one syllable, like a yawp or bark. In official Washington, the essential AARP is the sleek and imposing headquarters building, the confident splashes of multicolored marble inside the building lobby, the subdued elegance of the offices (not lavish, but spacious and efficient), the video production room, the well-stocked research center, the legions of energetic young researchers, lawyers, and policy analysts who people the halls. It is a $500 million-a-year organization, by far the largest lobbying group in the country, and one of the capital's biggest private employers. With 32 million members, it dwarfs almost all other membership organizations. Only the Roman Catholic Church with some 60 million members is bigger, while AARP and the American Automobile Association jockey back and forth for second-place honors.

In Washington, a city of perpetual gridlock, you earn respect by getting things done—anything done. In a perverse way, the Simpson Senate hearings signaled the respect that politicians from every part of the ideological spectrum have for AARP, however grudging it may be. A preliminary artillery pounding is a standard battle-opening tactic, and anyone serious about restructuring social programs for the aged, as Simpson is, must pay attention to AARP. In an age of grassroots politics, AARP's ability to energize local activists, to target political waverers in their home districts, to produce floods of written or video material on almost any subject, can be envied, feared, or admired, but never disregarded.

That is the image of AARP as seen through the Washington lens, but if the scale is shifted, the magnification of the lens adjusted a bit, an organization comes to light that is quite different from the lobbying legend.

Gail Chisholm is sixty, a former school administrator. She's about five feet tall with a pleasant round face, crisp brown curls, and brown eyes that snap with cheerful energy. It's a warm June night in Northport, New York, a leafy, salt-breezed town on the south shore of Long Island Sound. About sixty-five people are gathered on metal folding chairs in the un-air-conditioned auditorium of the local Veterans' Hospital, a postwar relic with polished wooden floors, dark-stained wainscoting, and hollow acoustics. Chisholm is holding forth at the podium on stage with the polished ease of a congressional candidate, congratulating the Northport chapter on completing its first full year and being officially certified as an AARP chapter. (Complimented later on her platform style, she smiles "I've been told that" without a blush.) After introducing her father-in-law from Florida, a frail man in his eighties who has been an AARP member for more than thirty years, and joking about two-generation AARP families, she turns serious and reminds the chapter members that they have obligations, and that their primary objective is to serve their community.

The people in the audience are mostly white-haired couples, but they don't look old. They're in their middle to late sixties, healthy, and tonight's mood is social—there is much calling out as new couples come into the room. The highlight of the evening is a square dance with a professional caller, so clothing runs to cowboy shirts, most of which look new. Unlike most AARP chapters, Northport schedules its meetings at night, because a number of members work. (Northport chapter members say that neighboring chapters are "older," which is why they wanted their own. But the turnout at a chapter meeting in neighboring Massapequa looks pretty much the same as at Northport. The frail old may not show up for meetings.)

After a lengthy installation of officers—there is a formal reading of the AARP bylaws because the chapter is newly certified—the president, Vic Pizzolato, a sixty-six-year-old insurance broker with a salesman's handshake, reminds the members that they can have front-row seats at a veterans' hospital fireworks display if they show up to help the disabled veterans with their wheelchairs. Sy Horowitz, a retired teachers' union official, gives a fiery speech on the Simpson hearings, warning that "the battle has started to save Social Security and Medicare." But the official chapter newsletter passed out at the meeting has a long reprint from a *Business Week* article warning that "greedy grandpas" defending their entitlements could impoverish their grandchildren. Peter Neglia, the newsletter editor, a retiree from an aerospace firm, says "you can't cry like a stuck pig" if benefits have to be cut. Horowitz says later, "We can all read the numbers and we know that something has to be done. But it has to be fair. You have to cut the farmers and the corporate welfare, too."

But the chapter meeting is not about Social Security and Medicare, and Horowitz's warning is the only mention of entitlements. It's a social occasion; a chance to get involved in volunteer activities; to hear reports on local problems, like security or property taxes; to hear speakers on investment programs, living wills, or custodian arrangements; and to find out about AARP programs and informational materials. (No AARP products were touted at the meeting, and the piles of AARP informational brochures did not include any AARP product literature.) Most of the people are there to meet their friends and have fun.

Chisholm organized the chapter because she had heard that Northport seniors were frustrated by the long waiting lists to get into neighboring chapters. She wheedled a meeting room from the local public library, ran off some announcements of an organizing meeting that she posted around the town, and was pleasantly surprised when more than forty people crowded into the meeting room. After Chisholm explained the basics, the group picked its most vocal members to be an organizing committee, and they formed the chapter at a subsequent meeting at her house. "I guess I opened my mouth the most, so they made me president," Pizzolato says a bit ruefully.

Chisholm is a professional, and she's good at what she does. Besides her organizing work, she supervises the training of all AARP volunteers in New York—

there are thousands. Personable, calm, and organized, she's quickly worked her way up the AARP hierarchy—this is her third job in as many years. And she works hard: She's on the road a lot, and has to stand up and perform in towns and cities all around the state at all kinds of hours. And she is not paid anything. "Whenever I get a promotion, they add a zero to my paycheck," she jokes.

AARP reimburses its volunteers for their out-of-pocket expenses, will pick up phone bills, or in some cases the cost of an extra phone, and pays gas mileage. But it has a full-time, or nearly full-time, professional labor force that does not ask for salaries. Gene Pritz was a department store executive who then ran his own public relations firm; now he works as the AARP state communications coordinator. Dick Keiser was the personnel manager for a manufacturing company and works the phones developing jobs for unemployed AARP members. Florence Katz was a computer programmer and is setting up the job bank for Keiser's hiring program. AARP volunteer jobs are not just handed out. They are posted through the AARP communications network. You have to apply, submit a résumé, and go through several interviews before being "hired."

AARP has 150,000 Chisholms and Pritzes and Keisers and Katzes in its "employ" all around the country, devoting ten, twenty-five, forty, sometimes sixty hours a week to AARP business. Only a handful of Fortune 500 companies dispose of a professional cadre as big, and no company can match them for dedication or loyalty. At AARP, there is no backbiting over salaries or bargaining over benefits, and it can operate with only a minimum of management infrastructure. Jurisdictions happily overlap, and the organization structure looks blurry and disorderly. But no other volunteer organization, including the Democratic and the Republican Parties, can marshal so large and unified a force in the field. And it is the permanent field force, not the money, or the small army of lobbyists, or the research and publicity resources of the Washington headquarters, that is the secret of AARP's power.

## AN OVERVIEW OF AARP

AARP was founded in 1958 by Dr. Ethel Percy Andrus, the first woman to become a high school principal in California, an idealist, and an organizational dynamo. She founded the National Retired Teachers Association, or the NRTA, in 1947 when she was forced to retire from her principalship upon reaching the age of sixty-five. And she was seventy-six when she created AARP as a parallel organization to bring the benefits of the NRTA to seniors who had not been teachers. That, at least, is the official story. Portraits of Dr. Andrus adorn the AARP corridors, and her stress on the service mission of AARP is cited with pride by members and with irony by the organization's critics. "A.A.R.P. holds no meetings to bewail the hardships of old age, nor to formulate pressure programs nor stress potential political strength of older folk, nor to urge government subsidy" is the classic Andrus quote.

The actual story is more complicated. Until the

early 1980s, the official "cofounder" of AARP was Leonard Davis, a young insurance agent who figured out how to create a group health insurance policy for NRTA members. Davis financed the creation of AARP, it appears, primarily to expand his own mail-order health insurance market; and for much of its existence, AARP was almost completely under Davis's control, operating as a sales network to hawk very high-priced insurance and a host of other Davis-created products to old people. I will explore the origins of AARP in more detail in the next chapter. Suffice it to say that, after becoming a very wealthy man, Davis was forced to break his ties to AARP in the early 1980s, and now seems to be something of a nonperson in the official organizational history. For the past decade, AARP has been trying hard to live down its early history, but the guilty ghosts of the past still occasionally rise up and cast their shadow, as they did fleetingly at the Simpson hearings.

Today's AARP is a nationwide enterprise, with about 1,700 paid staff. Some 1,200 people work out of the Washington headquarters, and about 300 are housed in Lakewood, California, along with the production offices of *Modern Maturity*, the organization's magazine. There are state AARP offices in twenty-one states, each with about a dozen employees, and the organization hopes to have forty-two state offices in place within a year or so, as part of a long-term plan to push more of AARP's resources and staff out from headquarters and into the field.

In 1994, AARP's operating revenues were $382 million. In addition, AARP received $86 million in federal grants to operate programs for seniors, for a grand total of $468 million. A single member pays $8 a year in dues and receives two publications—*Modern Maturity*, the country's largest-circulation magazine, a slick, full-color, bimonthly with a slant toward the problems and opportunities of aging; and the *AARP Bulletin*, a tabloid-style roundup of mostly Washington-based legislative and political developments of interest to seniors. The AARP membership card also makes members eligible for AARP discounts. About two dozen hotel chains offer AARP discounts, and Avis and Hertz discount their car rentals by 5 percent for AARP members.

The travel discounts seem to be the reason most people join. Fifty-year-olds, the minimum age of membership, don't naturally jump to join a "senior citizens'" organization without some inducement. Receiving the first membership solicitation from AARP, in fact, usually comes as something of a shock, but it is one from which almost no American is exempted. The sheer efficiency of AARP's direct-mail operations is legendary. Almost every American begins to receive mail solicitations to join AARP about six months before he or she turns fifty. The mailing operation is so thorough—try to find a fifty-year-old who hasn't heard from AARP—that it is widely assumed that AARP has access to Social Security records. In fact, the list is built from diligent mining of hundreds of data sources—drivers' registrations, credit card data, voter registration lists. It is an awesome, and expensive, operation that few other organizations could duplicate.

AARP has no choice but to concentrate aggressively on member solicitation. As an older persons' organization—two thirds of the members are over sixty-five, and about 2 million die each year—it has to run hard just to stay even. The graying of the boomer generation, the huge cohort of Americans born between the end of World War II and the early 1960s, is viewed with a mix of anticipation and trepidation. If the percentage of the fifty-pluses joining AARP stays constant, membership could double over the next decade or so. On the other hand, boomers are notorious nonjoiners, and membership rolls actually slipped slightly over the past year. In any case, for the great majority of members, sending in the $8 for the membership card, receiving the magazine and the newspaper, and picking up the occasional travel discount is the sum of their contact with the organization.

But AARP makes a lot of money selling things. Perhaps 20 percent of the members buy an AARP-labeled product, and the fees, royalties, and interest income associated with product sales accounted for 48 percent of AARP's 1994 income. About two thirds of the product income is from AARP's health insurance line, underwritten by Prudential, most of it supplemental insurance to back up Medicare. The remaining products are a mélange of housing, auto, and life insurance; mutual funds, annuities, bank cards, and mail-order prescriptions. The great rap against AARP during the Davis days was that AARP products were a rip-off. Although there are still a few dogs on the list, a fair assessment today would be that the products offer excellent values. In addition, every member is automatically eligible for most of the insurance and credit products, which makes them especially valuable for, say, widows who may otherwise have trouble purchasing insurance or establishing credit on their own.

There are thousands of other nonprofit organizations that pick up extra income by selling "affinity" products—for example, BASS, the Bass Anglers Sportsman Society, offers a line of boat insurance and engages in pro-fisherman lobbying—but AARP is the biggest by a vast margin. Not surprisingly, its sales activities prompted prolonged disputes with the Internal Revenue Service and the U.S. Post Office over the taxability of product revenues and the use of its nonprofit mailing privileges.

While not conceding any of the IRS's tax claims, AARP made a "voluntary" payment of $135 million to settle claims for back taxes covering the period through 1993, and made an additional payment of $15 million in 1994. Similarly, AARP made a $2.8 million back payment to the postal service in 1993 and now uses commercial rates for all its product mailings. (A complete review and evaluation of AARP's product offerings and a more complete description of the postal and IRS disputes appears as an Appendix on page 209.)

On the spending side, publications are the biggest single item in the AARP budget. AARP produces seventeen newsletters besides *Modern Maturity* and the *AARP Bulletin*, and a host of pamphlets, special studies, and even videos, most of them aimed at specialist audiences and addressing topics like aging and the law, women's health issues, volunteering, employment and aging, consumer alerts, and low-income housing. Total publications spending was a round

$100 million in 1994, offset by $47 million in advertising revenues.

AARP's next biggest spending item is member services and acquisition, which includes new-member solicitation and the design and supervision of AARP products. Then comes field services and programs, which include most of the volunteer activities and the network of state and area offices. Legislative activities, which include lobbying and the AARP policy research institute, cost about $35 million. Almost all the federal grant money goes to operate two community employment programs, mostly for low-income seniors. Most of the money goes directly for wages for program participants, and the AARP administrative expenses, at 14 percent, seem reasonable.

Simpson and others have questioned the propriety of nonprofits that engage in federal lobbying also receiving federal grants, although no one has suggested that AARP uses the federal money for anything but the narrow purposes of the grants. Both houses of Congress have passed legislation prohibiting nonprofits from receiving federal grants if they engage in lobbying activities. The legislation, predictably, has prompted outcries from a wide assortment of agencies and still hangs in the balance as this book goes to press.

AARP does not pay its executives eye-popping salaries. The executive director, Horace Deets, gets a yearly salary of $292,000 and a benefit package worth another $46,000. Nineteen other executives earn $100,000 or more. Deets's salary must sound like a lot of money to a retiree struggling along on Social Security checks, and federal cabinet officers don't get paid nearly as much, but executives running businesses of comparable size and complexity get paid considerably more than Deets, and Washington trade association executives typically get several times as much.

## AARP DREAMS

"Probably 80 percent of the attention that we get in the media has to do with our legislative activities," Horace Deets says with some frustration. "And another 15 percent is about our products and services. But that's not the bulk of our activity. We spend only 10 percent of our expense budget on legislative activities. Education, information, community service, and local advocacy, not just legislative advocacy, is the core of who we are." Deets has been with AARP for twenty years, starting out in educational volunteer programs and gradually rising through the bureaucracy until he was appointed acting executive director in 1989 and executive director a year later. Obviously very smart, he is highly articulate and has a good voice, but speaks in a slow, even tone that is bland and soothing. Before the Simpson committee, his patient, detailed, somewhat plodding answers were effective at dissipating some of the hostile atmosphere in the hearing room. When Deets talks about his service vision for AARP, he radiates an utterly convincing sincerity. A former Catholic priest, he has the air of a committed idealist, with perhaps just a touch of the zealot.

Deets's frustration at AARP's typecasting is understandable. The community service and information programs really do constitute the vast bulk of AARP activities and consume by far the greatest proportion of staff and organizational energy. But the truth is that AARP's social activities would be of little interest except to the participants and beneficiaries themselves were it not for AARP's leverage over legislative issues of national importance.

It is no coincidence that AARP's political profile has risen to such prominence precisely in step with the growing realization that the country's biggest public policy challenge is the financing of income and health security for the aged. AARP will be a key player in resolving that challenge, and its service ambitions not only speak to the organization's self-perceptions but say a great deal about the attitudes, the values, and the preconceptions that it brings to the debate.

Deets has a vision, and when he speaks of it a quiet fervor creeps into his usually bland delivery. Deets envisions AARP as the nerve center of a national network of older Americans dedicated to tackling the country's social problems—caring for or protecting the dependent aged; spearheading community improvement initiatives; reaching out to deprived children as mentors, tutors, and caregivers; revivifying the political process. He speaks glowingly of Sr. Isolina, an eighty-five-year-old nun in impoverished Ponce, Puerto Rico, who, out of her community's own sparse resources, has created an artisanal training center and workshop and a computer school—all based on respect for the individual and helping people do for themselves, says Deets feelingly.

To Deets's credit, the core AARP workers, from

Anne Harvey, the program head in Washington, down to state and local staff and the "professional volunteers" like Gail Chisholm and Gene Pritz, preach more or less the same line, that AARP is about doing things for other people, and not necessarily just for the old.

The biggest AARP service programs are Tax-Aide and 55-Alive. In 1994, some 31,000 Tax-Aide volunteers provided tax assistance to some 1.5 million low-income aged, including house calls for shut-ins. Seven thousand 55-Alive volunteers provide driving skill upgrading and defensive driving techniques for more than half a million seniors. (There is an $8 charge for the course, and it generates about $5 million in income. The IRS puts up $3 million for Tax-Aide, most of which goes to volunteer expenses.) Other organizations run the same tax and driving programs, but AARP's are by far the biggest, and demonstrate its unique organizational skills.

The list of laudable AARP undertakings extends to quite a considerable length. Widowed Persons' Services provides counseling and support groups for the recently widowed—115,000 in 1994—all run by volunteer counselors who are themselves widowed. A women's breast cancer initiative is a concerted, nationwide effort to convince older women of the importance of mammographies. The program involves an awareness campaign backed up by a number of publications, volunteer training, and a professionally prepared video that is available to AARP chapters and other local organizations.

AARP has recruited and trained some 2,000 volunteers to assist state nursing home ombudsmen. (A recruitment drive in one state started with a mailing to 900,000 seniors, who were finally winnowed down to 54 trained volunteers.) A grandparents' initiative focuses on the mare's nest of legal issues—like emergency room release forms—that might confront grandparents who find themselves raising their grandchildren. Retired lawyers provide legal services to seniors in a number of cities, and AARP is training senior paralegals to help with specific recurring legal problems, like housing or disability payments.

Perhaps the most attractive new program is AARP Connections for Independent Living, in which AARP places its communications network at the disposal of *other* senior citizens agencies. In New York City, AARP committed to delivering volunteers for a series of programs sponsored by the city's Office on Aging. A telemarketing firm called thousands of people in targeted zip codes. People who responded favorably got follow-up mail and came in for a briefing and interviews. AARP gave the city the names of several hundred prescreened, qualified, and willing volunteers. "When we first started AARP Connections for Independent Living," Anne Harvey says, "we were worried about losing the AARP identity. But in fact local agencies have asked us if they can use the AARP logo to advertise that they're part of our network." The telemarketing campaign also demonstrates how AARP can leverage small amounts of money and its unmatched senior marketing data base to turn out volunteers in ways few local agencies could ever do by themselves.

By the end of the decade, Deets hopes that AARP's

computers could maintain volunteer directories and service resources for every community. "You should be able to call up an 800 number and get pointed to a local service you need or an opportunity to help out." The idea may be impracticable, even a bit grandiose, but it says a good deal about AARP's vision of aging in America.

## VISION AND MONEY

If a single word were to characterize the AARP vision for older Americans it would be *freedom*. Freedom from want, freedom from fear—fear of catastrophic health crises, fear of dependence on children or cold professionals—at least for as long as possible. Older people will keep their homes, live comfortable well-socialized lives, and, AARP hopes, use all that spare time to do useful things for the rest of the community—mentoring children, being there for the failing aged, providing examples of wisdom and service for younger people.

At least as far as their material well-being, the AARP vision probably matches pretty well with what older people want for themselves. The organization's surveys show that 85 percent of the over-sixty-fives want to "age in place"—that is, keep their homes until the last possible moment. Older people, unfortunately, are probably not as unselfish as Deets would like them to be (who of us is?). A lot more AARP members head for the slot machines at Atlantic City than turn out for volunteer calls. But that is just another aspect of freedom that few would begrudge. AARP surveys show that younger people share the same vision of a desirable state of aging as older people do.

In fact, it would be hard to imagine *anybody* quarreling with the AARP vision of a decent life for the elderly if it weren't for the unpleasant question of how much it will cost. A substantial portion of the elderly, indeed, probably a majority, have already achieved something like the AARP vision, which AARP doesn't dispute, although they rush to quash the growing notion that the old are rich. A good many of the elderly actually are well off, but many are still disgracefully poor and even larger numbers just barely scrape by. At the Northport chapter meeting, Chisholm remarked, "Nobody here is really worried much about their future. But there's a real difference with the older aged. People start to panic when they can see the possibility of a nursing home or Alzheimer's."

Many other Americans, however, are also poor, and also have worries about their future. And the cost of providing benefits to the aged is rising alarmingly, particularly the cost of health care as the relentless march of technology opens a cornucopia of therapies to smooth the aging process—hip replacements, arterial bypasses, corneal and cochlear (hearing) implants. The system of benefits is a strange patchwork of too much and not enough. Many benefits are paid to people well able to get along without them, even to the very wealthy; but one must become impoverished before the government will pick up the cost of an extended stay in a nursing home. To make matters worse, starting in about twenty years, the number of the aged will begin to rise very sharply as the baby-boom generation starts to retire. If one projects present trends that far ahead, there's just no way the numbers work.

And that is why AARP is suddenly controversial. Over the next several years, resolving the question of aged benefits, and the kind of retiree lifestyles the rest of the country can afford to pay for, will dwarf virtually all other public policy issues. As the premier spokes-organization for the aged, although not nearly so unchallenged as it once was, AARP will be a major player in that debate. And in that context, the formidable volunteer lobbying network that AARP has developed will be far more important than its services programs.

But before looking at AARP's lobbying power, it would be well to air some of the skeletons that still shadow its reputation as a disinterested broker for the old.

# Chapter 2

## *The Gorilla's Somewhat Questionable Past*

LEONARD DAVIS IS A Palm Springs multimillionaire who doesn't like talking to journalists, or even having his picture taken. The few newspaper photos available show a forceful-looking man with silver hair, horn-rimmed glasses, and a wide, strong mouth that turns down at the corners. Davis has a somewhat checkered past. He was once indicted for perjury, although he was acquitted at trial. (The judge in a nonjury trial said that the indictment was "entirely justified," but found that the prosecutor had fallen short of the "reasonable doubt" standard.) And after the New York State Insurance Commission brought a charge of "untrustworthiness" in 1968, Davis agreed to surrender his insurance license, without admitting the charge. But Davis was a direct-marketing genius who virtually invented the business of selling insurance through the mails. When he retired from his business activities around 1981, estimates of his personal fortune ranged as high as $200 million. By the end of the decade, Davis was drawing dividends of as much as $5 million a year. Socking away a couple of hundred million in the 1970s vaulted him into the ranks of the richest men in America, among the very crème de la crème of the seriously wealthy. Davis made his money by selling through the mails to America's elderly, and the organization he created to hawk his wares was AARP.

Davis was already a successful insurance broker in Poughkeepsie, New York, in 1955, at the age of only thirty-one, when he met Ethel Percy Andrus. She had already launched a convalescent village and a retirement home for her teachers, but her great frustration was her inability to arrange private health insurance for her members. This was the pre-Medicare era, and teachers usually lost their fringe benefits on retirement. Insurance companies simply did not sell health coverage to people over the age of sixty-five, and over the years, forty-two companies turned her down—they thought she was some kind of "crank," she said. But as Andrus traveled around the country cultivating her fledgling organization, she heard of Davis, who had worked out an insurance plan with Continental Casualty Co. for a group of retired teachers in New York. Andrus tracked him down, and Davis developed a similar policy for Andrus's teachers, one that could be sold through the mail. The policies sold by the tens of thousands, and since the teachers turned out to be good risks, who paid their premiums on time, they were very profitable.

Andrus and Davis were quickly besieged by other retired people, who were not teachers but who wanted to buy health coverage. So Davis put up $50,000 in cash in 1958 to finance the founding of a parallel organization that he and Andrus called the American Association of Retired Persons. (AARP and the NRTA were officially merged only in 1982, although they always functioned as a single operation.) By 1963, the AARP and NRTA membership rolls had ballooned to 750,000 and the insurance business was booming, so Davis bought out Continental's AARP/NRTA policy business in order to keep the profits himself.

There is no suggestion that Andrus ever viewed AARP as primarily a business proposition. She does not appear to have gotten rich from the enterprise, and she always stressed its idealistic mission as a self-help organization. She was already elderly when she met Davis, and she died in 1967 at the age of eighty-five. From its very inception, the empire that AARP eventually became was shaped by Davis's driving business ambition.

From the outset, Davis cultivated AARP's most powerful marketing tools—its famous mailing list and its publications. Most of Davis's initial investment of $50,000 apparently went to fund the creation of *Modern Maturity*, and on the very first page of the very first issue was "Invitation to Security"—a message from Andrus about health insurance. The *Bulletin* began the process of positioning AARP as the most powerful lobbying voice for the aged. Once again, it was a shrewd stroke. Identifying AARP as the reliable advocate of the aged in Congress would vastly enhance the credibility of its sales offerings.

Davis's initial business ideas were undeniably good deals for his members. Until he showed the way, health insurance was simply not available for older people. The first year after AARP was founded, he and Andrus created what was arguably the first mail-order pharmacy business in the country, Retired Persons' Services (RPS). He induced a series of big retail druggists to join the RPS system of filling prescriptions by mail. Since the mail-order operations generated large volumes, and could be carried out in cut-rate space, RPS users could buy drugs at substantial discounts. And 1 percent of all sales flowed into the AARP coffers. Mail-order drugs is now a big business, but RPS is still one of the very few that sells at a retail level.

By the early 1960s, Davis had organized his business into a series of companies operating under the umbrella title of the Colonial Penn Group. Colonial Penn Insurance sold AARP members a full panoply of health, life, car, and homeowner insurance policies. Colonial Penn Travel ran the travel service. Mature Temp Services, a Colonial Penn subsidiary, operated a for-profit employment service for oldsters. There was even a Colonial Penn trailer park for the elderly. (Only RPS was independent of Colonial Penn.) Stock analysts estimated that about 80 percent of Colonial Penn's revenues, and "substantially all" of the health insurance revenues, came from AARP/NRTA members.

At AARP conventions, the Colonial Penn products displays and booths were interspersed with the booths dispensing advice on diet and exercise programs for older people, and on AARP community service and educational operations. AARP's much-touted defensive driving programs for the elderly were used to sell Colonial Penn auto insurance. The insurance sales pitches in *Modern Maturity*, like "Thinking Positively and Planning Ahead" (June/July 1976), were framed to look like advice articles. One expert on marketing to the aged called the AARP/Colonial Penn setup "the slickest mass marketing scheme I've ever seen."

Although the Colonial Penn companies were theoretically separate from AARP, Davis, to protect his marketing bonanza, wrapped Colonial Penn tentacles firmly around every aspect of the AARP operation. According to a 1977 lawsuit by a former executive director, Harriet Miller, Davis had carefully insulated the board from AARP's financial operations, and at the same time had made them almost utterly dependent on Colonial Penn. Contracts drafted for AARP by lawyers close to Davis, for example, delegated the right to select insurance carriers for AARP and NRTA members to a private company called National Association Plans, Inc.—a subsidiary of Colonial Penn.

In the early 1970s, Davis shored up his control by introducing a new law firm as AARP's outside counsel. The firm, which went through several name changes, maintained offices in the same Madison Avenue building that housed Colonial Penn's New York offices, AARP's local offices, and Davis's personal offices and those of the Davis family foundation. Three principal partners, Lloyd Singer, Al Miller, and Cyril Brickfield, were close Davis associates. Singer, in fact, was a key Colonial Penn executive who had been at various times president of the Colonial Penn life insurance company, chief executive officer of the entire Colonial Penn Group, and president of another Colonial Penn subsidiary, CPG Data, Inc., which performed extensive services for AARP. Brickfield, whose name was on the law firm's nameplate, had actually become executive director of AARP in 1967, at Davis's recommendation, but had stepped down to legislative counsel in 1970. He resigned in 1975 to take over the Miller, Singer Washington office, and came back again as executive director in 1977, after the disruption of the lawsuit. He retired only in 1987, reportedly receiving a seven-figure severance bonus.

As if to squelch any doubts where control lay, the AARP board elected Davis its "honorary president" in 1967, and the executive committee stipulated in 1977 that Davis should "provide it . . . on a regular basis with the benefit of his financial, accounting, and management expertise . . . ; Leonard Davis and such associates as he selects shall have full opportunity to meet with the Association personnel; and the staff shall cooperate to the maximum extent."

The volunteer AARP board members seem to have been easy to manipulate. Meeting agendas were developed by the outside lawyers; the lawyers kept the minutes and, according to the Miller lawsuit, casually rewrote or "fabricated" what had gone on. In the words of Alice VanLandingham, AARP president from 1976 to 1978, outsiders were kept in line with petty privileges. The Colonial Penn insiders, the "group," as she called them, "wine and dine the national officers, board members. When any one of them questions anything, they are individually taken out to lunch." Key staff members were closely tied to Colonial Penn. One member complaint submitted to a 1976 board meeting was:

> I am of the opinion that no employee of Colonial Penn Group or affiliated organiza-

> tion(s) should be given staff or leadership roles in NRTA/AARP. This opens us up for criticism of self-perpetuation of interests, e.g., Ruth Lana, Tour Services; Leonard Davis, Honorary President; Marion Rossilli, Membership. The two should be divorced completely. There are other examples of this dual role.

And another was:

> Why can't NRTA/AARP enjoy the services of its own exclusive Legal Counsel which is completely separated from the Colonial Penn Group? Example—Lloyd Singer and his relationship with the Nominating Committee. I cannot accept his role in counseling the Committee and his absolute control of the Committee functions. . . . This relationship is unsound and unwise. It appears to be unsavory based upon established business practices and organization.

More important than lunchtime flattery or petty manipulations was the utter control of AARP operations. The famed AARP mailing list was maintained and controlled by CPG Data, Inc.—that is, all mailings to AARP members went through the hands of a Colonial Penn company. When members complained to VanLandingham about the volume of AARP product solicitations they received with her signature on them, she pleaded that she had never seen the letters until she received them herself. And Davis was very generous with his advertising and royalty payments to AARP. A glossy AARP magazine, a highly visible lobbying program, striking and useful service operations, the ability to blanket the country with membership solicitations and to offer a glittering array of benefits at apparently nominal cost—in short, a strong and effective AARP—meant a bigger and bigger captive market for Colonial Penn products.

The real question was what kind of a deal were members getting from the products they bought through AARP. Some individual offerings, like the mail-order pharmaceutical business, undeniably saved money for oldsters. But Davis's success quickly produced a host of competitors, and his insurance offerings, the heart of the Colonial Penn business, were mostly very poor. A 1974 Senate subcommittee investigation into mail-order life insurance policies found that, of 119 policies analyzed, Colonial Penn's ranked "close to the bottom" of the list. Pennsylvania insurance commissioner Herbert Denenberg said that life insurance was a waste of money for most older people with limited incomes and few obligations. Other large senior organizations either stopped their life insurance programs or recommended that their members not buy any. *Money* magazine analyzed the AARP Medicare supplement, or "Medigap," policy in 1975 and found it the worst but one in the universe that it sampled. A Blue Cross policy, for example, that cost $6.62 a month paid $92 per day for the first sixty days of hospitalization, and $23 per day thereafter, and also paid for skilled nursing home care after twenty days in the hospital. The AARP policy, for almost the same premium—$6 as opposed to $6.62—paid *no* benefits for the first week of hospitalization, only $20 per day from the eighth through the sixtieth day, and $30 per day thereafter, with *no* skilled nursing home coverage. Nursing home coverage was available for an extra monthly premium of $5.75, making the total AARP charge 77 percent higher than that of Blue Cross with a much more anemic range of benefits. (Today's AARP policies withstand such comparisons much better.)

It didn't take an insurance expert to figure out why the AARP premium/benefit ratio was so poor. For every dollar that Blue Cross took in, it paid out 93 cents in benefits. But for every dollar that AARP took in, it paid out only 62 cents in benefits. Of the remainder, about a nickel went to AARP, and the rest, or 23 cents, was retained by Colonial Penn. A 1975 study by the California insurance commission found that the Colonial Penn payout ratio in that state was only 53 percent, just barely over the regulatory minimum of 50 percent, and far lower than the 86 percent payout of a comparable Blue Cross policy.

Colonial Penn defended their low payout rates by arguing that they were selling individual, retail policies, which imposed much higher selling costs compared to competitors selling through employer groups. But at the same time, Colonial Penn's chairman bragged to stockholders that their "cost-effective distribution system" resulted in a "low acquisition cost level . . . unmatched by any company of which I am aware." Finally, it didn't hurt that all the solicitations on the AARP letterhead, like those purportedly signed by VanLandingham, went out at nonprofit postal rates, less than a third of what other insurance companies would have had to pay.

A scathing report in the January 1976 issue of *Consumer Reports* reviewed, in much greater detail than *Money* had, sixteen different Medigap policies, including Colonial Penn's flagship health insurance product, and found that "Taken as a whole, the AARP (and NRTA) policies offer the least protection." Even worse, *CR* included a full-page inset that blasted the relationship between AARP and Colonial Penn, detailing all of Davis's AARP-dependent businesses, and showing how:

> money flows from NRTA and AARP members into the coffers of Colonial Penn . . . [and] money flows out of those coffers to pay NRTA-AARP. . . . Members of NRTA and AARP are privy to few details of the intricate financial and organizational ties that bind the senior associations to Colonial Penn. Once a year the associations publish their financial statements for member inspection. Colonial Penn is not mentioned by name. . . . Colonial Penn's promotional material appears as editorial matter in NRTA-AARP publications. The promotions are listed in the table of contents as articles. . . . Members of NRTA and AARP doubtless assume that the two nonprofit associations act as disinterested arrangers of the services they endorse . . . [but] should be aware that the endorsement of various

> Colonial Penn products by the organizations reflects a cozy commercial relationship, not a disinterested selection among similar services that may be available.

The public relations problems would have been more manageable if Colonial Penn had not been making so much money. AARP, which to all appearances was a dowdy nonprofit organization serving the elderly, had been turned into a money-minting machine—it was the alchemist's trick, said one reporter, converting "base metal into gold." From 1967 through 1976, Colonial Penn's revenues had grown a stunning tenfold, from $46 million to $445 million. Pretax income had grown from almost nothing in 1967 to more than $50 million. Almost all of its revenues—92 percent of its health insurance revenues—came from NRTA/AARP members. An analysis by *Forbes* magazine in 1976 showed that Colonial Penn, measured by average five-year return on capital, was the most profitable company in the country. (Not the most profitable *insurance* company in the country, but the most profitable *company*.) All of which adds point to this excerpt from a Davis address to the 1966 AARP national convention:

> Let me preface what I am about to say by making a very personal digression. It has been my privilege, and yes, even honor to have been a counselor to this organization since its inception, and to have seen it grow and prosper. . . . But most of all during this time, *I have obtained a heightened sense of my*

> *own personality and potentials thanks to my contact with all of you.* [Italics in original.]

Although he had retired from the chairmanship while still a young man, Davis was active on the Colonial Penn board and, with about 19.5 percent of the stock, was the controlling stockholder. The market value of his shares, depending on the ups and downs of the stock market, fluctuated between $90 million and $125 million in 1975 and 1976. And that did not count the large blocks of stock Davis had already unloaded. In 1970–72 alone, the Davis family realized more than $80 million from the sale of Colonial Penn stock.

Revealingly, it was precisely the points that bothered the *Consumer Reports* editors that made eyes sparkle on Wall Street. A Loeb Rhoades analyst pointed out that Colonial Penn's health insurance was "written predominantly on a fixed-indemnity basis," meaning that Colonial Penn paid a flat amount per hospital day rather than a percentage of the actual cost. "As such," the analyst went on, "it has proven not to be so much affected by the upward spiral of inflation as more typical accident and health plans." From the consumer's standpoint, of course, that meant that the value of the benefit was steadily eroding. The ties with AARP virtually insulated Colonial Penn from the violent zigs and zags of the 1970s economy. A Smith Barney analyst enthused in 1976, "The Company has never had a disappointing earnings year or quarterly earnings report since going public in July 1968. Very few companies can match that record."

"The Company's symbiotic, unique relationships

with two older age associations," the Smith Barney analyst concluded, "provide it with both a semi-captive market and third-party endorsement of its product line unmatched by any other insurance company in sheer size of its potential insureds." The major risk the analysts foresaw was an outbreak of "Consumerism" à la the *Consumer Reports* article, which was viewed as a major negative event, but they were confident that Colonial Penn could weather such storms.

Colonial Penn's success, and Davis's wealth, were also starting to be noticed by the more astute AARP members. A 1976 member complaint went:

> In view of the high ratio of earnings by the Colonial Penn Group, why couldn't the premiums and other charges . . . be reduced to really effect a savings for the membership? Why can't Mr. Davis be satisfied with a net worth of 50 million dollars instead of the alleged 300 million?

Other senior publications began to air complaints about AARP's high-pressure sales tactics:

> We are constantly being bombarded with sales pitches for the "AARP Insurance Plan". . . . It seems that a new letter comes almost every two weeks.
>
> This is the type of letter the AARP keeps sending me. I do have an in-hospital policy. Now they've sent me this other in-hospital

> plan policy which would raise my policy to $19 a month. I pay $10.50 a month. How can a retired person on a fixed income keep raising monthly payments? Ever since I belonged to AARP they have been sending letters for more insurance.
>
> My husband and I are in our eighties and we are members of AARP. We have received dozens of circulars on Colonial Penn's "AARP In-Hospital Plan" so we dispatched the $12 premium for both of us. Recently the enclosed circular (covering another In-Hospital Plan) has been received, completely confusing us. Do we have the coverage we need? Are the others better? Is there some hitch?
>
> I have become more and more dissatisfied with AARP. . . . It bothers us that AARP is bringing out new small policies repeatedly. There is one to cover surgery, another for accidents, etc. This seems to me to be very confusing and in the long run more expensive. . . .

The Hawaii chapter of the NRTA passed a resolution to investigate the Colonial Penn relationship, and to award the insurance contracts by competitive bids. When NRTA president Mary Mullen became alarmed about the spreading revolt in Hawaii and another one in California, she wrote to Lloyd Singer and Al Miller to warn Colonial Penn about the seriousness of the problem. Implicitly, that is, she treated Singer and Miller as if they represented Colonial Penn as much as NRTA. The lack of competitiveness in the AARP policies was defended, "feebly" in the view of *Forbes*, by executive director Harriet Miller: "It's not exclusive. It's just that nobody else is approved by our board."

Lawsuits stirred the pot further. A 1977 class-action suit and an antitrust suit failed on technical grounds. A much more serious legal action was the one by Harriet Miller, who was ousted from her executive directorship in 1977, after less than a year and a half on the job, for it threatened to split AARP. Miller was an owlish-looking social activist, and an experienced politician and lobbyist, who for several years had been in charge of AARP's lobbying activities. (She is now the mayor of Santa Barbara.) Miller contended that, once in the job, she gradually became aware that the Colonial Penn relationship was not in the best interests of AARP members. She thought that representations being made to postal inspectors about the noncommercial nature of AARP mailings were simply not true. When she tried to carve out a course of action independent of Davis's representatives, she was harassed, overloaded with petty assignments, and eventually ousted from her job.

VanLandingham backed Miller's contentions. As early as 1976, she complained in a letter to the other volunteer directors of "childish dirty tricks," and of her shock to discover that the very first election she had been involved in was a "fixed frame-up." A 1978

VanLandingham letter on the Miller suit, however, addressed to "Those of you who care about the Future of AARP," was much stronger:

> I feel it is important and necessary for me to send along this Memo. I understood the great purpose that Dr. Andrus had to have on behalf of older people. . . . Together, we can do our part to save the American Association of Retired Persons, for those who shall follow us. Your help is needed, now!
>
> . . . My last two years have taught me much. . . . Not until I was president did I realize the in-house games being played by the controlling GROUP.
>
> . . . The Honorary Presidents [there were two, Davis and the tour director, Ruth Lana] interviewed each member of the Executive Committee, individually, and convinced them that Harriet was unfit and they had letters to prove same, which was ridiculous and shameful. They grilled me for four hours and I never agreed with them.
>
> Harriet's Suit is not against the Associations and if any of you can support her at this time, write her . . .

AARP settled the Miller suit out of court, paying her $480,000. One of the stipulations of the settlement was that the court records be sealed. Even today, Miller says, her lawyers have cautioned her not to talk about AARP. Although the pot was bubbling, the lid was still on.

As often as not, it is the random events that turn out to be decisive. In 1977, Andy Rooney, of CBS's *60 Minutes*, was one of the most trusted journalists in the country, with an audience many times bigger than that of narrowly focused, semitechnical journals like *Consumer Reports*. Rooney, whose face still reddens with anger when he recalls his investigation into AARP, was taping "some typical Washington bureaucratic story" in 1977, and needed an outside shot. His crew picked a bland marble Washington office building on K Street that had the kind of broad, open entrance expanse to frame the shot they wanted. They did not know it was the AARP office building, and Rooney himself had never heard of the organization. "But when we started shooting," Rooney says, "all kinds of people came running out of the building saying we couldn't shoot there, which was ridiculous, because we were on the sidewalk. They acted like they had something to cover up. I decided right there that I was going to find out more about them."

The *60 Minutes* exposé of AARP, which aired on May 14, 1978, at the seven o'clock prime-time news hour under the title "Super Salesman," was devastating. A former Colonial Penn executive remembers it as a "turning point" in the company's fortunes. AARP and Colonial Penn made all the wrong tactical moves. They tried stonewalling Rooney, refusing to let officers and directors speak with him, and making him and his crew cool their heels for three days at an officers' convention without an interview. Rooney retaliated, of course, with a classic "empty chair" interview. (In any case, AARP national officers, fed up with the Colonial Penn domination, were quietly feeding Rooney information and rumors.) An AARP official who finally granted an interview to deny influence by Davis insisted on holding it in his own office, which was dominated by a framed oil painting of Leonard Davis. The AARP volunteers and members Rooney did manage to talk to clearly had no idea of the role Colonial Penn played in their organization. Most tellingly, AARP members had no idea that editorial-like articles on health insurance in *Modern Maturity* were actually Colonial Penn advertisements.

A centerpiece of the show was an interview with E. French Dennison, a retired air-conditioning engineer whose hobby was making ceramic tiles. Dennison was one of the insurance trustees who were supposed to oversee the purchasing, pricing, and management of the AARP insurance programs. Although AARP later claimed that Rooney had taken Dennison's remarks out of context to make him look bad, the complete transcript of the interview makes it clear that Dennison was in no position to counterbalance the influence of Colonial Penn. Typical exchanges were:

*Q. Do you periodically review competitors' claims that they can give you better insurance than Colonial Penn can?*

*A.* Oh, yes, yes, we do that.

*Q. When was the last time you looked into anything new?*

*A.* We—we meet at least twice a year. And sometimes more—more often.

*Q. And competitors enter bids.*

*A.* Oh, no, no. No, there isn't any of that.

***Q.*** *Why not?*

***A.*** Well—well, because we have the—this setup with our organization that we're perfectly happy with, and we don't find any need for it.

***Q.*** *Do you know much about insurance?*

***A.*** No, and I ask—when I want anything, I ask the insurance people. (Laughs.)

***Q.*** *You mean you trust the people at Colonial Penn?*

***A.*** The—the people that I know, and I know them, of course, all very personally. . . . I have just never met a finer group of people.

The Rooney show marked the beginning of the end of the Colonial Penn/AARP relationship. In a related development, the postal service had begun a serious investigation into the Colonial Penn/AARP use of the nonprofit mailing privilege. AARP insisted that the investigation was just a "routine thing," but a postal investigator stressed on Rooney's show that "it's not a routine check. It's an in-depth study that's been going on for two years." In fact, the investigation continued until 1981 and resulted in a recommendation to the U.S. district attorney for a criminal fraud action against AARP and Colonial Penn. The district attorney declined to prosecute because of the difficulty of proving criminal intent.

With exposés, lawsuits, and member disaffection swirling on every side, Davis finally permitted Singer and Brickfield to orchestrate a gradual disentanglement of Colonial Penn and AARP. The flagship sales product—the group health insurance—was finally bid competitively in 1981, and awarded to Prudential Insurance, who promised a much higher benefit ratio for members. All of the other Colonial Penn programs followed suit. Davis officially retired from involvement with Colonial Penn in 1983, and a Florida utility bought out the company shortly thereafter, while Davis settled in Florida to concentrate on his extensive philanthropic activities. Shorn of its profitable AARP connection, Colonial Penn quickly fell into serious financial difficulties, and for a while its survival was in question. In an ironic twist, the company, now on the outside, brought an antitrust suit against AARP in 1985 for its refusal to allow competitive advertising in the pages of *Modern Maturity*. AARP itself suffered temporary financial difficulties in the early 1980s, partly because the bills for Andrus's retirement villages began falling due. One response was to reduce the membership age from fifty-five to fifty to increase the pool of potential member/customers.

Although Colonial Penn's fingerprints stayed on the organization for a long time—the Singer law firm was not completely phased out until the 1990s, and Brickfield ran the organization until 1987—the organization began a serious redirection in the mid-1980s. Few of today's senior staff were even at AARP during the Davis days. While Andrus's picture is everywhere, and she is quoted frequently, I could not find a single mention of Davis anywhere. The former honorary president, whom the official histories once billed as Andrus's closest collaborator, is now a nonperson.

Pressing older staff about the Colonial Penn years usually draws only a curt, "That was a long time ago."

And, to be fair, the Davis years *were* a long time ago. Although I approached the product reviews (see the Appendix) with extreme skepticism, most of them turn out to be good values, and some are the best available. The worst accusation one can level today against Deets and the AARP staff is that they are "the field artillery in a liberal army," as the *Wall Street Journal* once put it, which is often true enough, but there are more heinous human failings.

The most striking change, perhaps, has been in AARP's lobbying activities. Although it is not fashionable to say so, AARP has gradually emerged as one of the more responsible of Washington lobbying organizations, and for the 200+ million Americans who are not members of AARP, it is AARP's lobbying activities that will have the most influence on their lives.

# Chapter 3

## *The Gorilla at Work*

MARCY CREQUE IS A very pleasant-looking African-American woman with iron-gray hair, a self-assured platform presence, and a grandmotherly air that inspires instant trust. The firm "Good morning" that opens her presentation is an echo of her career as an AT&T customer service manager. Creque is a "professional" AARP volunteer from Chicago, but her stage is a Catholic church basement in Worcester, Massachusetts, where some two hundred senior citizens have gathered on a warm summer's morning in 1995, amid sprays of red and white balloons and a scattering of nervously hovering youthful AARP staffers, to "celebrate" the thirtieth anniversary of Medicare.

The occasion is part of a thirty-city roadshow somewhat hastily cobbled together by AARP as a consciousness-raising exercise in anticipation of the fall congressional battle over cutting back the growth of the program. "I've been running all over," confesses Susan Able, thirty-five, the legislative assistant for the six-state AARP Northeast region, who is struggling with the logistics of the celebrations—like mounting a program in a steeply pitched auditorium in Paterson, New Jersey. (No one fell, Able sighs.)

The Worcester event offers a three-dimensional slice of the complicated reality of AARP—the awkward combination of amateurism and professionalism, of stump-style rabble-rousing and Deetsian civics-book earnestness—and demonstrates the deep seriousness with which older people treat Medicare. The turnout is a little disappointing to the AARP staffers, who were hoping for three hundred. But the room looks crowded, and local television and National Public Radio are there, so the event is chalked up as a success. Surprisingly enough, the program starts almost exactly on time and ends when it is supposed to. The first half hour is given over to local speakers—the thirtysomething mayor of Worcester delivers a dais-thumping political speech ("You've worked for Medicare *all your lives*!"); a recovering cancer patient laments looming cutbacks ("Next they'll be talking about euthanasia!"); and a black minister with a gospel-style delivery recites a poem about never quitting the fight.

Then a panel of four traveling AARP volunteers, including two national board members, take over. They open with a slickly produced videotape on the history of Medicare—clips of World War II, and America saving the world for democracy; Harry Truman's failure to win a health insurance bill; fast cuts of booming factories and giant reapers on the Great Plains; John Kennedy and the New Frontier; Lyndon Johnson signing the Medicare bill and handing the first pen to a tearful eighty-one-year-old Harry Truman.

Creque's presentation is the heart of the program. It is a carefully balanced statement of the predicament facing Medicare, set out in a clear, classroom-primer style. The hospital trust fund *is* facing insolvency in 2002, but that has been true on at least twelve previous occasions. Congress has always modified the program to bring spending back in line, and will do so this time, too. The amount of savings required to bring the hospital trust fund into balance through 2005 is $110 billion. But the Republican budget proposal calls for $270 billion in Medicare cuts through 2002, so the cuts are deeper than needed just to save Medicare. AARP believes that Medicare must be brought into balance, she says, but should not be used to solve the rest of the deficit problem as well. (She does not get into the huge deficits facing the system when the baby boomers start becoming eligible in about 2013.)

The highlight of Creque's program is a forum-feedback session on Medicare alternatives. With the help of a Washington-based AARP technician, she outlines the four options that are under discussion in Washington, from charging more to the wealthy to a complicated voucher plan. Handouts spell out each alternative and list the pros and cons of each. Young staffers with microphones encourage audience members to state their opinions. Creque asks everyone to fill out feedback questionnaires and turn them in at the end of the program.

Creque is resolutely balanced throughout. When the audience shouts "Yes!" on the question of cutting provider payments, she patiently explains that many doctors are withdrawing from the program because of low Medicare payments. A woman complains about

Medicare premiums and deductibles, which Creque counters with an anecdote about bypass surgery to show how expensive modern procedures are.

The audience proves itself extremely well informed on the operating details of the program—one woman asks if it's true that Medicare is using their money to subsidize teaching hospitals (it is true). But many seem confused by the reform alternatives, especially by the voucher proposal. Although a large number of people fill out the feedback sheets, it would be hard to know what to make of them. Overall, the session nicely illustrates the wholly admirable AARP commitment to political education and the limitations of participatory processes for complicated issues.

The program ends with a flourish. Senator Ted Kennedy has sent a videotape, so a screen is rolled down onstage. A huge round image of the senator's face materializes over the crowd like the Wizard of Oz and delivers a rip-snorting attack on the Republican cutback program. Lou Pare, the local volunteer AARP political coordinator, points out the tables in the back with writing materials to send a message to congressional representatives. (AARP does not use form letters—they believe officials ignore them—but will mail the handwritten letters.) There is a Medicare birthday cake, a senior singing group is belting out "Heart of My Heart," and Pare announces that a delegation will bring some cake down the street to the local congressman's office and ask him to "Cut Cake, Not Medicare." Amid much cheering and waving of signs, a couple of dozen people head for the congressman's office.

As the meeting breaks up, Able is visibly relieved

that it has gone well. She admits to having worried about the partisanship of the Kennedy speech. "We invited everybody, of course," she says, "but Kennedy was the only one who responded, and he asked if he could send a tape. We said okay, but don't make it partisan. But the tape was clearly pretty partisan, so we thought we wouldn't use it. Then we discussed it with Washington, and it seems there have been a lot of meetings where only Republicans came and bashed the Democrats just as hard, so on balance they decided it was okay. I was a little uncomfortable though."

Able's, and AARP's, fastidiousness are not likely to be typical of the Medicare debate. A full-page ad that the Republican National Committee ran in July features a tombstone with the epitaph "Medicare 1965–2002" along with a "Republican pledge to preserve, protect and improve Medicare." The implication that Medicare will have to *end* in 2002—"Medicare won't be there to help"—is not true, as is the statement that the Republican budget program is "saving Medicare." (The Medicare trust fund will have $150 billion in revenues in 2002, but revenues and accumulated assets won't be enough to cover projected outlays.) A House Republican Conference advisory for candidates' meetings with seniors suggests focusing on fraud and abuse:

> Ask your constituents to write to your office with their accounts of abuse and also devote the first fifteen minutes of your meeting to "fraudtoids". . . . The same people who believe eliminating foreign aid will balance the budget also believe that eliminating

> waste, fraud, and abuse will solve the Medicare problem. For seniors, the government may be the enemy, but the real emotional venom is reserved for doctors and hospitals. . . . Everyone has a story or complaint.

The Republican position, however, is more honest than the paleoliberal argument. Kennedy's tape promises that if fraud and abuse are ended, there will be no financial problems, which is simply untrue.

## THE POLITICAL NETWORK

The Worcester "celebration" was sponsored by AARP/Vote, nominally in alliance with other area seniors' agencies, but with AARP/Vote clearly in the steering position. AARP/Vote is the grassroots advocacy and political education arm of AARP. Although it comprises only a small minority of the AARP volunteers, it is AARP/Vote that politicians are thinking of when they speak of AARP as the "eight-hundred-pound gorilla" of politics.

AARP's political advocacy activities date from its very founding. AARP/Vote, however, is a relatively new organization, dating only from 1986, designed to push more of the advocacy activities out into the field. Like most AARP activities, it is a virtuosic exercise in the marshaling of volunteer people power. Every state has a volunteer AARP/Vote Coordinator, who oversees a system of district coordinators—one for each congressional district—and district teams of volunteers.

District teams range in size from five to twenty people, with a target average of eight. In bigger states, there are layers of volunteer specialists between the state office and the districts. California has more than five hundred AARP/Vote volunteers, with about thirty-five working at the state level, serving, for example, as legislative specialists and communications coordinators. There are currently some two thousand trained volunteers in place in state and district teams, with a full staffing objective of about thirty-five hundred by 1997 or so. The volunteers are supported by a dozen Susan Ables—paid staff spotted around the country to assist in training volunteers, researching policy issues, and maintaining liaison with the policy and lobbying chiefs in Washington.

Much of AARP's formidableness derives from its ability to back up its volunteers with professionals and to come up with the money to finance events and mailings. The oldest state coordinator is Paul Franklin Bliss, the volunteer head of AARP/Vote in Rhode Island. Eighty years old, a retired minister with snowy white hair and a Mark Twain mustache, he points with pride to the Rhode Island AARP *Voters' Guide.* Published for each major statewide and national election, it is a compendium of candidates' positions on key issues, much like League of Women Voters publications but with a particular slant to senior issues. (Voters' guides are "clean" publications, with no AARP advocacy statements, to avoid jeopardizing its status as a nonprofit political education organization.) At various times, AARP has financed the publication of up to a quarter million guides, which are mailed to all Rhode Island members, and in the 1994 election inserted them in the main state newspaper as a special Sunday advertising supplement.

*Guide* publications are big-ticket undertakings, but it is the small amounts of money that give AARP a reach that other volunteer organizations can only envy. The Worcester affair, Able estimated, cost $6,000–7,000, mostly for a mailing to twenty thousand local members. (The 1 percent turnout is a normal response.) In the mountain states, AARP has financed candidate night satellite television uplinks so the debates can be carried on local public television. An AARP-financed local cable television debate in the 1992 California Senate race between Barbara Boxer and Bruce Herschensohn cost only about $8,000, but it was eventually seen by some 2.5 to 3 million Californians, because it was picked up by cable stations around the state. The professional backup also gives the local AARP volunteers an edge over other activists. One of the standard functions of district teams is to meet regularly with local congressmen and other officials. The legislative assistants, like Able, will arm them with AARP research and role-play the interviews so the volunteers can sharpen their questions and practice pursuing evasions. (Many of the volunteers, however, are former union or government officials, and have considerable legislative or lobbying experience themselves.)

Despite the decentralization efforts, AARP/Vote is still very much a Washington-driven organization, and "activating the grass roots," in AARP jargon, is almost always a Washington decision. Jim Butler, the Washington AARP/Vote director, and a former teachers' union organizer, guesses that he "turns on the network" twenty-five to thirty times a year, although he rarely uses the entire network at one time, preferring targeted strategies. AARP is trying to develop stronger state-level programs, but has been less successful. One problem is that outside of the big-ticket, Washington-based entitlement questions, there are relatively few issues that generate a natural consensus among AARP members. In both New York and Rhode Island, for instance, grassroots anti-local-tax sentiment among AARP members has bumped heads with the strong teacher influence in AARP.

AARP counts the defeat of the Balanced Budget Amendment in 1995, which doomed a key part of the Republican "Contract with America," as a major legislative success, and it is a classic demonstration of the AARP lobbying technique. Since there was little hope of defeating the amendment in the House, where Speaker Newt Gingrich disposed of a disciplined majority, AARP concentrated on the Senate, and especially on about a half dozen "waverers," like Wendell Ford of Kentucky and Joseph Biden of Delaware. (To AARP's great disappointment, Biden decided to vote for the amendment; Ford stayed opposed.)

In the last days of the debate, as the preliminary vote count hovered right at the required two-thirds majority, AARP focused its efforts on the two senators from North Dakota, Kent Conrad and Byron Dorgan—look-alike conservative Democrats, both business school graduates and former state tax commissioners, and among the last remaining senators not to have taken a position. North Dakota is a conservative state, where the voters instinctively favor balanced budgets. Both men were publicly agonizing over their choice. Dorgan had voted for a Balanced Budget Amendment the previous year, and was considered a crucial vote by Republican leaders. Conrad had voted against the previous year's amendment, and was not counted in the majority's column, but he was known as a deficit hawk. He called his vote "the most important vote I may ever cast in the United States Senate" and refused to be stampeded into a decision.

The AARP strategy was twofold: to demonstrate sufficient support for a "no" vote in North Dakota to allay the senators' fears of being punished for voting against the amendment, and to provide a salable intellectual defense for a negative vote. The first part was easy, just a matter of the AARP machine swinging into action. "Telephone trees" were activated throughout the state. When a "tree" is turned on, each AARP volunteer starts making phone calls to a list of people who are asked to call the target's office, and to call other friends to make similar calls. Within hours, the two senators' switchboards were flooded with thousands of calls. Mass mailings went to every AARP member in the state asking them to call or write in favor of a "no" vote. Rallies were held in the state capital. AARP spokespeople were logged onto local radio and television talk shows. A full-time AARP staffer was dispatched to Bismarck to be sure the campaign went smoothly. "We mobilized all over the landscape," says Butler. When Dorgan and Conrad eventually voted the right way—they admitted to being almost overwhelmed by the "no" vote partisans—the same process was repeated to "give them a big round of thank-yous and support to show our appreciation."

The intellectual defense was harder. There are reasoned arguments against the amendment—that it imposed too rigid a limitation on congressional action, that congressmen are paid to make choices, that the amendment was merely a cynical ploy that the majority had no intention of enforcing—but none are terribly appealing. The argument that wavering Democrats like California's Dianne Feinstein and Senate minority leader Tom Daschle of South Dakota, and eventually Dorgan and Conrad rallied around was that the balanced budget calculation should not count the Social Security trust fund surpluses. It was a perfect sound-bite argument, complicated, confusing, and with the ring of rectitude. "All we asked was that we not rob the bank to pay the debt," said Daschle.

It is also intellectually incoherent. Between 1995 and 2002, the Social Security trust funds will take in about $470 billion more than they will pay out. (The system flips into massive deficits when the baby boomers start to retire.) Congress, technically, is not supposed to count those funds in calculating the annual budget deficit, but they do, which makes sense, because the money is invested in government bonds and therefore produces cash to fund current operations. By insisting on *not* counting the surpluses, the AARP/Democrat position would have required even *bigger* budget cuts to achieve a balanced budget—instead of the $1.2 trillion in cuts targeted by the Republicans over seven years, the goal would be raised to almost *$1.7* trillion. In cash terms, the government would be required to run a $470 billion surplus over the period.

Neither AARP nor Feinstein, Daschle, Conrad, or Dorgan really believed that the government should be running surpluses. This was a time when AARP was trumpeting the danger of excessive budget cuts. Raising the budget deficit hurdle would make it *more* likely that Social Security and Medicare payments would be cut, which is the last thing AARP wanted. The Social Security argument was just a confusing smoke screen, a way to throw sand into the Republicans' Balanced Budget Amendment machinery. Since AARP regarded the Balanced Budget Amendment as a cynical ploy to begin with, they countered with a cynical ploy of their own to defeat it.

The Conrad/Dorgan exercise was a much higher-profile effort than most AARP lobbying efforts, but it illustrates the AARP strategy of careful targeting. "We light up the entire network once or twice a year at the most," says Butler. Early in 1995, there was a nationwide call-in campaign in support of Medicare shortly after the new Congress arrived in Washington. "We began to hear from them around the middle of the day to ask us to call off the dogs," says Butler. "We just wanted to make sure that they knew we were around." The bread-and-butter of the AARP lobbying program, however, are much smaller issues, the host of little government benefits for seniors scattered throughout the budget: energy assistance for low-income heating and air-conditioning bills; low-income elderly housing programs; consumer protection laws; the grab-bag of programs funded through the Older Americans Act—funding for state offices for the elderly, funding for the nursing home ombudsman program, and a host of others. The lobbying and the telephone tree–type exercises almost always focus on committee votes, and target just the handful of legislators whose votes are likely to be decisive.

All in all, the impression is of a skilled, highly professional organization with smooth coordination between the Washington lobbying arm and the grass-roots network. Such a formidable machinery, however, makes it all the more important to be clear on what AARP stands for.

## THE TWO POLICY FACES OF AARP

There are two distinct policy faces of AARP. With respect to Social Security and Medicare, the national AARP office is one of the most responsible of all Washington lobbying organizations. Listening to the national officers like Deets, John Rother, the legislative policy director, or Martin Corry, the chief congressional lobbyist, discourse on the major entitlement programs, one is impressed with the careful nuances of their positions, their willingness to face hard choices. Like Marcy Creque's session in Worcester, positions are carefully drawn, factually based, and accurately presented, in welcome contrast to those of many, perhaps most, other senior organizations.

But with respect to almost all other issues, the bread-and-butter details that account for most of the actual AARP lobbying effort, the organization is relentlessly statist. Judging by its formal legislative agenda, it never saw a government program or a government regulation it didn't like. The official AARP legislative program is a telephone book–sized tome prepared each year in a marathon session involving the top couple hundred AARP volunteers and the core staff. It is an unabashed celebration of what the British call the "Nanny State," a drab vision of a fanny-patting, spoon-feeding government with a vast centralization of regulatory authority in Washington.

The impression is of a seriously schizoid organization. In its Personality One version, AARP is assiduously educating its constituency in the difficult trade-offs facing Social Security and Medicare. But when Personality Two takes over, AARP resolutely sets its face against ever making any choices at all, or worse, it wants to shift all the choice-making power to bureaucrats in Washington.

***AARP as Realist*** To appreciate the refreshing contrast between the primary AARP lobbying positions and those of many other seniors' organizations, consider this statement made at a 1995 congressional hearing by James Martin, the head of 60/Plus, a seniors' organization "of a free enterprise, less government, and less taxes philosophy," resolutely in favor of a balanced budget amendment:

> We stress Seniors' issues such as: (1) repeal of the so-called Federal Inheritance Tax, a job-robbing, punitive double tax on the savings and earnings that Seniors plan to leave to their heirs; (2) repeal of the increased tax on benefits of Social Security recipients . . . ; (3) repeal of means testing

> on Seniors; (4) raise earnings limits on Seniors [to qualify for Social Security benefits] in fact not only to raise, but to do away with it.

This is the sheerest hypocrisy. Martin is saying that he is willing to bust the federal budget to put as much money as possible into the hands of seniors, especially those who are financially better off. Let somebody else shoulder the spending cuts and the taxes. It takes breathtaking chutzpah to wrap paeans to balanced budgets around such a "gimme" philosophy.

One of the best litmus tests for hypocrisy is the "Notch." The newsletters of seniors' organizations like the National Committee to Preserve Social Security and Medicare regularly feature stories of "Notch Victims," and some of the most vocal balanced budget advocates, like Senator John McCain, have regularly voted to "repair the Notch." The "Notch" is one of the more arcane nooks and crannies of Social Security law. In the 1970s, Congress and the Nixon administration passed very sharp increases in Social Security payments. In their haste to award new benefits in an election year, the legislation incorporated arithmetic errors that resulted in larger increases than had been intended. Congress was forced to address the errors a few years later when spending threatened to run out of control. In a compromise, people who had already qualified for the extra benefits were allowed to keep them. People becoming eligible over the subsequent five years kept part of the extra benefit on a sliding scale, and all later retirees followed the benefit schedule originally intended. The second group, of course, are the "Notch Victims," tirelessly agitating for the same unintended bonus their predecessors received.

AARP has consistently opposed fixing the "Notch," because no one was ever entitled to the extra benefits, and the trust funds can't afford them. For the same reason, it has opposed eliminating the Social Security earnings exemption—the system can't afford it, and the money will mostly go to those least likely to need it. (They would like to raise the present exemption ceiling, however.) AARP was also the only seniors' organization to maintain its support for charging seniors for the cost of the 1988 Medicare Catastrophic Care bill—the principle of "pay for what you get," in Alan Simpson's words. It did not lobby against a 1993 tax increase on Social Security benefits to help fund Medicare, although it could have killed the tax if it had wanted to, and it is, as far as I can find, the only seniors' organization to offer reasoned options for reducing Social Security benefits to bring the trust funds into long-term balance. (The United Seniors' Association, a conservative group, is working with the Republican congressional majority in devising ways to rein in the Medicare program.)

In each of these cases, AARP has passed up the opportunity for winning cheap applause from its members in favor of the more difficult, but more responsible, position. Its willingness to look facts in the face, and to take responsible positions grounded in the data, are its primary claim to credibility in Washington.

With the exception of Alan Simpson, few of the current cast of AARP-bashers could pass a similar hypocrisy test. McCain's positions on Catastrophic Care and the Notch make him one of the leaders of the legions of Forked-Tongues. To his credit, Simpson is one of the few conservative legislators whose positions are consistent: He publicly favors balanced budgets, and is just as publicly willing to trim senior entitlements to get there. It is interesting that, despite Simpson's recent attacks on AARP, he and AARP have more often been on the same side of issues, as they were on the "Notch" and the Catastrophic Care bill, than the other way around. This is the AARP Personality One in action.

***The Nanny State AARP*** But when one turns to the AARP national legislative agenda, one confronts the other AARP, Personality Two. There is none of the same concern for costs or excessive spending, none of the same reasoned trading off between the desirable and the possible.

The official AARP legislative agenda is in favor of more spending on almost everything—on AIDS; on mental health, home health care, and prescription drugs through Medicare; on expansion of state Medicaid criteria to include more near-poor elderly; on long-term care; on nursing home training; on expanded state Medicaid, nursing home, and mental health programs; on increased social services in the community and in nursing homes; on supplemental income programs and food stamps; on the national senior service corps; on housing assistance for the aged; on the homeless; on rent vouchers; on older farmworkers; on public housing; on energy assistance; on legal services; on virtually any activity ever funded through the Older Americans Act; on poor children; on productivity improvement; on worker education;

on worker adjustment services; on rural health care; on poverty amelioration; on gerontological research; on cleaning up the environment; on industrial research and development. At the same time, AARP wants to cut budget deficits to increase national savings.

The Personality Two AARP is one of the last true believers in the salvific power of government regulation. It wants more regulation on age discrimination and the arbitration of claims; on the rights of the disabled; on private employer retirement, compensation, and termination practices; on requiring state provision for employees without health insurance; on health insurance rates; on HMO standards; on health care fraud and abuse; on health care quality standards; on requiring physician performance data; on drug prices and drug patents; on hospital diagnostic standards and procedures; on Medicare patient access; on home health care outcomes; on Medicare appeals; on manufactured housing standards; on consumer rights to utility services; on funerals; on night clothes and space heaters; on condominium sales. There are dozens more, including that hoar-frosted relic of the diehard Old Left—rent control. The only regulations AARP doesn't like are those that prevent elder communities from keeping children out of their developments.

Personality Two likes centralized government. It opposes converting the Older Americans Act into state block grants, because it would limit the impact of centralized AARP lobbying. It wants the federal government to regulate smoking, cemeteries, and crematories. Just as God liked beetles, AARP likes plans—

consolidated state housing plans, plans for housing the frail elderly, state social service plans, food stamp outreach plans, long-term care plans, assisted living plans, state health care plans. It is fond of "interagency coordination"; it wants federal standards for almost everything; it likes data banks, surveys, information systems, centralized reporting. At the same time, it wants to reduce "unnecessary paperwork." The legislative agenda, in short, is a window into the mind of the apparatchik run amok, a paean to paperwork, a vision of a bureaucrat's nirvana—endless rows of desk-bound gray suits holding meetings, writing memos, and checking forms.

The list of AARP national officers offers a clue to the statist enthusiasms. They are, of course, all accomplished people, but two thirds of the twenty-one national board members are retired public school teachers or government employees. There are seven teachers, six former government officials, and one woman who was both a teacher and a public health nurse. The remaining seven comprise two doctors (only one of whom was in private practice; the other was the medical director of Exxon), an academic economist, and only four people with primarily business backgrounds, two of whom, from Lockheed and the Bell system, are from companies used to a high degree of government regulation.

The 1994–95 board president, Eugene Lehrmann, is a former vocational education teacher and administrator from Wisconsin; the previous president, Lovola Burgess, is a former teacher and high school principal from Iowa; while Margaret Dixon, who will be the 1996–97 president, is a former New York City elementary school teacher and principal. As one might expect, their reaction to almost any problem is that government should step in, and the legislative agenda reads as if it were written by a "National Association of Retired Public Employees," not by an organization claiming to represent all older persons.

AARP staffers tend to become exasperated when they are criticized about the legislative policy agenda. "It's just a wish list," said one. "Nobody expects it to be enacted." (The National Taxpayers' Union claims that the policy agenda would cost a trillion dollars. In fact, there is no way to make such a calculation, since the policy agenda is mostly in the form of exhortations with few fiscal specifics.) But the statist instincts start at the top. In explaining the AARP position against the Balanced Budget Amendment, for example, Rother said in the *Bulletin*, "It poses a very serious threat to the economy and to the benefits that people depend on—everything from farm subsidies to veterans' benefits as well as Social Security and Medicare." The implication that AARP supports farm subsidies truly suggests that there is no subsidy it would not favor.

Assistance to the aged, especially to the aged who are both frail and poor, is the most defensible of all government undertakings. There are no worries about sapping initiative; no one thinks the poor aged should get off their duffs and go to work. But even assistance to the most deserving has to be tempered by considerations of affordability and limits. It may not be possible to provide nursing care for everyone who needs it, and at the same time to engineer a vast upgrading of nursing care standards, desirable though that might be. Ensuring that all the aged get decent health care may require limiting their choice of doctors and procedures. The paleoliberal, big-government, tax-and-spend, never-make-a-choice style of governing occupies a diminishing political ground. By so flagrantly parading its statist reflexes in its annual policy exercises, AARP makes itself a deserving target for Republican fire, and undermines its own ability to play the role of honest broker in a national debate about Social Security and Medicare.

AARP should be a uniquely important resource in the continuing process of reforming entitlement programs. It has substantially reformed itself over the past decade, and the exploitative marketing practices of the Colonial Penn days ended long ago. The tax settlement with the IRS, while not yet final, holds the promise of closing those chapters entirely. Its service accomplishments, allowing for all exaggerations, are real and respectable. The volunteer organization is a strikingly effective tool for public education, political participation, and community improvement activities. AARP's research is outstanding, and it has become one of the most reliable and comprehensive sources of information on the attitudes of the aged and their problems of daily living. No other organization can match its ability to communicate en masse to older Americans, and despite some fraying of its reputation around the edges, probably no other organization is as trusted by seniors. The reputation of its lobbyists on Capitol Hill, even among conservative staffers, is still quite high, all disagreements admitted.

The split personality of AARP, however, will be a major handicap in realizing its potential as a reliable purveyor of research, an unbiased spokes-organization for aged concerns, a trustworthy communications channel to the mass of its membership. To the extent that AARP allows its Personality Two version to dominate, to the extent it represents the attitudes only of people who have spent their lives on public payrolls, it will become merely another remnant of the shrinking forces of the paleoliberal left, and can expect no more attention than that position deserves.

A critical early reform would be to ensure that its national officers match up better with America's seniors. People whose career advancement and salary increases have always depended on a legislative vote—at bottom, on raising someone else's taxes—will inevitably view the world differently from people who had to struggle to come up with the taxes, meet their payrolls, and keep their businesses going. With the narrow experiential base of its top officers, AARP can't truly claim to represent its 30+ million members, which is a shame, because it is in a position to play a key role in the greatest issues of our time. Restructuring the AARP board so that no more than a third of the members came from the public sector, and at least another third had run their own businesses, would be a good start.

AARP has become such an important political player, however, only because of the unprecedented salience of senior issues, especially Social Security and Medicare. Those are the issues we turn to in the next section.

# II

# *What's at Stake*

# Chapter 4

## *Senior Entitlements Under the Microscope*

In the long view of American history, each era is defined by just one or two national policy issues—civil rights and social opportunity in the 1960s, inflation and energy in the 1970s, the confrontation with the Soviet Union and the end of the cold war in the 1980s. The defining issue for the rest of this decade, and well into the twenty-first century, will be the question of how America should provide for its aged. Government payments for cash pensions and medical care for the elderly are already equivalent to about 10 percent of the entire national income, and they will grow rapidly over the next decade or so to account for about half of every dollar spent by the federal government. But that's not the bad news. In about the year 2010, the first wave of the baby boomers will start to retire—this is the huge age cohort that was born between 1948 and 1964, when America's fertility rate was its highest in modern history. From that point, the numbers get much worse. If one makes just a handful of pessimistic, but perfectly plausible, assumptions, it can be easily shown that income support and medical care for the aged will consume half or more of all payrolls in thirty or forty years. Such forecasts, of course, are absurd if they are taken seriously as forecasts. But they *do* show the scale of the problem and the necessity to start making decisions soon.

## AMERICA AND ITS AGED

The explosive growth in entitlement programs for the aged, and the ever more pessimistic financial forecasts, are driven as much by social developments as by financial and legislative decisions. In his 1934 Message to Congress on the original Social Security legislation, Franklin Roosevelt observed that "Security was attained in the earlier days through the interdependence of members of families upon each other. . . . The complexities of great communities and of organized industry make less real these simple means of security."

In traditional societies, parents lived with their children when they grew older, and if they became incapacitated they were cared for at home, usually by housewife-daughters. The traditional system was breaking down even in Roosevelt's time, and is on the verge of complete disappearance today. Most married women are employed outside the home, and are no longer available to provide nursing care for bedridden relatives. The high rate of family mobility in present-day America, as often as not, means that parents and children live in different parts of the country and see each other only infrequently. Substantial increases in the life span of the elderly mean that parents often do not become dependent until their children are in their fifties, or even sixties, perhaps struggling with college tuitions or worrying about their own retirements.

Advances in medical technology have greatly increased the mobility and the spending power of the aged. At retirement villages, it is routine to see eighty-year-olds on their second hip replacements playing golf. Cataract surgery, bypasses, aggressive physical therapy after injuries, antiarthritic drugs, revolutionary advances in prosthetic devices, along with much greater health consciousness—exercise, diet, not smoking—allow people to lead active, engaged, independent lives well past the Bible's allotted threescore and ten. Simply observe the energy and aliveness at any AARP chapter meeting.

Progress does not come without cost, and it is obviously very expensive to provide more generous pensions and much higher levels of medical care over much longer life spans. But there is an even darker side to the gains. Long periods of independent living after retirement create a frightening *de*pendence on institutional caregivers when body and mind finally begin to fail. If people are much less likely to keel over from heart attacks in their sixties, they find themselves instead vulnerable to chronic diseases like Alzheimer's in their eighties. Middle-aged sons and daughters, even those who love their parents and who have phoned and visited them faithfully over the years, panic at the prospect of an incapacitated eighty-year-old moving into their homes. For all practical purposes, America did not have a nursing home industry much before the later 1960s.

When one speaks about Social Security and Medicare to the older aged—people in their mid-seventies and beyond—the fear of nursing homes and Alzheimer's hangs over the conversation like a shadow. These are people who have been in charge of their own lives for a half century or more, and they are in quiet terror at the possibility of being removed from their homes, stripped of their assets, and warehoused as public charges amid a swamp of incontinence and senility. As I will show in the next chapter, the present generation of retirees, like all post-Depression generations before them, get far more financial value from the Social Security and Medicare systems than they paid in. But programs to shore up the American system for retirement support that do not provide for the end-stages of life miss a very large point. The fierce protectiveness of the comfortably well-off old for their Social Security and Medicare benefits is not just "greed." Under present arrangements, there is almost *no* level of asset accumulation plausibly within reach of a middle-class retiree that will provide peace of mind that she can traverse a prolonged end-stage illness with dignity and relative comfort in her own home, or at least at a site of her own choosing. These are fears that don't easily translate into economic terms, and they go far to explain why old people sometimes appear irrational in defending their benefits.

As I hope to show in this book, while the future of senior entitlements presents a very serious public policy problem, the biggest we face, it is not an insoluble, overwhelming crisis. Sensible, piecemeal, practical reforms implemented over the next three to five years should be able to bring the system into a reasonable long-term balance once again. Long delays in addressing the basic issues, however, could make the problem much more serious than it need be.

There are in the main three different government programs that protect the aged:

- Social Security proper is the much-tinkered-with Roosevelt-era program of cash transfers to the old, as well as to the blind and disabled. It is *not* in fiscal crisis. For the moment, in fact, it is overfunded, but not at a level that can sustain the retirement of the baby boomers at the present schedule of benefit increases.

- The second is Medicare, a Johnson-era Great Society program, which operates as a federal national health insurance policy for the aged. Although Medicare coverage restrictions have been imposed by every Congress over the past decade, spending has grown very rapidly and the program *is* facing insolvency. Without major policy changes, the Medicare hospital trust fund will not have enough cash to pay all of its claims in about six years—well before the boomers start to retire.

- Finally, there is Medicaid, passed the same time as Medicare. Medicaid is usually considered a "welfare" program—families receiving Aid to Dependent Children, for instance, are automatically covered by

Medicaid. But about a third of Medicaid spending goes for people over sixty-five, and more than half of all nursing home beds in the country are financed through Medicaid. Medicaid, technically, cannot have a fiscal crisis because it is financed by general revenues. Taxpayers put up whatever the program costs. But it is now almost as big as Medicare and stands second only to Medicare as a source of health care support for older people.

## THE PATCHWORK SYSTEM I: SOCIAL SECURITY

More than 90 percent of all workers are in jobs covered by Social Security. Benefits are financed by a payroll tax of 12.4 percent, half paid by the employer and half by the employee. The self-employed pay both the employer and employee portion of the tax. The first $61,200 of wages was subject to the tax in 1995, and the amount is increased each year based on a formula. An additional payroll tax of 2.9 percent supports the Medicare program, bringing the total employer/employee payroll tax to 15.3 percent. There is no limit on the wages subject to the Medicare tax. The payroll taxes are paid into separate trust funds. Surpluses are invested in government bonds at market interest rates.

Most economists agree that the employer share of the payroll tax should be treated as if it came from the employee's pocket. Since employers view the tax as a payroll expense, it may be presumed that wages are reduced by an amount roughly corresponding to the amount of the tax. The payroll tax is also a notoriously regressive tax—that is, one that falls with disproportionate weight on lower-income workers, since it is imposed on the first dollar of payroll income at a flat rate for all workers.

For a household with average income, the payroll tax, including the employer's portion, is almost two-thirds larger than their federal income tax liability, and largely offsets the income tax's progressive structure. In 1991, for example, a household with a median income paid an effective income tax rate (i.e., after deductions and exemptions) of 9.2 percent, compared to the effective rate of 15.0 percent for a household with twice the median income. But when the payroll tax is taken into account, the effective tax rate on the two households was almost identical—24.5 and 25.6 percent, respectively.

The regressivity of the tax is only partially counterbalanced by a payment formula that is skewed to provide a greater benefit-to-taxes ratio for lower-income workers. Social Security payments normally begin at age sixty-five, assuming the recipient is earning no more than a specified, low level of wages. (Retirement areas like Florida, as might be expected, are notorious for cash-based part-time employment.) Payment levels are set in three bands, for low-, average-, and high-wage workers. In 1995, the basic monthly benefit for a high-wage worker was $1,105; for an average-wage worker, $792; and for a low-wage worker, $480. Relative to their contributions, however, lower-wage workers still get the better deal. The 1995 monthly benefits represented 60 percent of preretirement wages for the average low-income worker, but only 34 percent for the average high-income worker. (See Appendix II for details of senior benefit programs.)

### *The Social Security "Contract"*

Social Security, until very recently, has always operated as a more or less pure "pay-as-you-go" system. The first generation of beneficiaries received far more benefits than they had "earned"—a worker retiring in 1940, on average, fully recovered his payroll taxes plus accrued interest in about six months. Benefit payments were never intended to be supported by the retiree's accumulated payroll taxes, in the manner of a true insurance or pension plan. Instead, the payroll taxes collected from working people cover the benefits paid out to the current generation of retirees. The implicit contract in the Social Security system has always been that each working generation pays for the current generation of retirees, and will be provided for in turn by the next generation of workers.

The point bears repeating because it is the subject of much confusion. Social Security benefits are not "earned" in an actuarial sense. Payroll tax collections are not earmarked into a special fund for each retiree, like an IRA or a 401(k) fund. If retirees had been allowed to invest all of their and their employer's payroll tax payments into, say, long-term Treasury bonds, and reinvest the interest, their accumulated nest eggs would *not* cover the Social Security benefits they are entitled to under present law. And, as we will see, the mismatch gets much worse when Medicare coverage is factored in.

The Social Security contract is that Generation A

collects retirement benefits from Generation B; and that Generation B should make the payments without complaining, because they will receive the same treatment from Generation C. Generation B has "earned" their benefits, perhaps, in a moral sense—they have done what was asked of them and could claim that they are entitled to their share of the bargain—but they have not paid for their benefits in a way that would make sense to an economist or an actuary.

The persistent trend of retirees getting more from the system than they paid in is reflected in the steady rise in payroll tax rates. From the 1950s into the 1990s, the total payroll tax rate increased by roughly three percentage points a decade, while the pay base subject to the tax was steadily increased in real terms, as workers struggled to keep pace with the steady rise in benefits conferred on new each generation of retirees. At the root of the present-day controversies over the system's future is the question of how long that engrained cycle of rising benefits and rising taxes can be sustained.

The relatively smooth rate of payroll tax increases over the years creates an illusion of an orderly process, a steady scaling up of benefits, perhaps, to accord with increases in national wealth. Like most government programs, however, it was nothing of the sort. The smooth averages conceal a disorderly lurching between extremes of beneficence and neglect.

## *Restructuring the System—the 1970s*

One of the great embarrassments of America's 1960s War on Poverty was the discovery that the largest number of poor Americans were not Appalachian cabin dwellers or minorities in urban slums but old people living on Social Security. Payroll taxes had been kept low over the years by paying a fixed Social Security benefit level that was only occasionally increased by special act of Congress, until Richard Nixon and a Democratic Congress massively liberalized the system in 1973 and 1974. Over the two years, benefit levels were raised by about 35 percent, and they were indexed for inflation. From that point on, benefits were automatically increased each year to keep pace with the Consumer Price Index, or CPI. The automatic adjustments are the famous COLAs, for Cost-of-Living Adjustments. The legislation was passed in such a rush, to win political credit (Nixon, at one point, tried to put the Republican logo on the checks containing the announcement, but Congress passed a law to stop him), that the formulas inadvertently increased benefits much faster than inflation. The worst anomalies were repaired in 1977.

The benefit increases, and the COLAs, were enormously successful in lifting the nation's old people out of poverty. It was arguably the most successful antipoverty program in American history. Between 1966 and 1974, the poverty rate among the elderly was cut in half, and today, with Social Security accounting for more than a third of their cash incomes, America's elderly are actually less likely than nonelderly to be poor.

The 1970s reforms, however, left a serious mismatch between benefit levels and payroll taxes. In the first place, the aged population was growing much faster than demographers had expected, because of declining death rates, and because people had begun retiring earlier. Then wages stagnated, even as inflation increased very rapidly. The automatic COLAs therefore pushed up benefit levels faster than payroll taxes. By 1981, it was obvious that the system was plunging toward a financial crisis.

## *The 1983 Restructuring*

After all attempts at reform through conventional channels collapsed in partisan wrangling, President Reagan and the Congress appointed a bipartisan commission chaired by Alan Greenspan. The Greenspan Commission's recommendations were passed by the Congress in 1983 and govern the system at the present day. These were major reforms. They mandated a series of sharp annual increases in the payroll tax and in the amount of covered wages; required almost all remaining uncovered groups, like state and local employees, to join the system in order to expand the wage base; froze COLAs for six months to pick up a one-shot cash infusion; provided for a gradual increase of the normal retirement age from sixty-five to sixty-seven by the year 2027; and made half of the Social Security benefits of the better-off old subject to income taxation.

Under the Greenspan reforms, the system's financing was shifted from a more or less pure pay-as-you-go basis to a semiactuarial system to anticipate the looming retirement of the baby boomers. The Social Security trustees now must forecast benefit levels and payroll taxes seventy-five years in the future and report annually whether income will exceed outlays over the entire period.

The system forecasts both its "long-term" actuarial status—the seventy-five-year period—and its "short-term" actuarial status—the next ten-year period. There are three projections: an "Intermediate" case, a pessimistic "High Cost" case, and an optimistic "Low Cost" case. The Intermediate cases are usually treated as gospel, although they have tended to be too optimistic in recent years. The 1983 reforms put the system into both short-term and long-term actuarial balance on the Intermediate projections—that is, through the year 2057, or the full seventy-five-year period.

### *The State of the Trust Funds*

One of the consequences of a semiactuarial system is that it will accumulate surpluses in years when the number of retirees is growing slowly in order to use those surpluses in periods when the population is growing rapidly. The retiree population is growing very slowly in the 1990s, so the system is now taking in much more money than it is paying out. By the year 2004, the system will have accumulated an incredible surplus, measured in constant 1995 dollars, of more than $1 *trillion* (!), a sum that will be equal to some 10 percent of total GDP (gross domestic product). The surpluses will continue to grow to a peak of about $1.5 trillion in about 2019. But even the huge surpluses looming ahead are not as big as expected, and they will be used up much faster than the 1983 projections assumed, simply because the life expectancy of older people is growing much faster than assumed and the wage base is growing much more slowly.

Assuming the present system of taxes and benefits is unchanged, the system now forecasts that the annual outflow of benefit payments will exceed income from payroll taxes starting about 2013, but that interest payments on previous surpluses will keep income and outgo in balance for about six more years. From that point, the trust funds will begin to eat into their surpluses. Huge as they will be, they will be quickly exhausted, and the trust funds will be insolvent by about 2029. At that point, retirees' annual legal claims will exceed the available annual resources.

The projections become much worse if one assumes that the Intermediate projections are too optimistic, as many scholars do. Only twelve years ago, in 1983, official Intermediate projections showed that the system was fully funded through 2057. Since that time, the annual forecast updates have moved the insolvency date almost thirty years closer. One of the most important variables in the forecast calculations, for example, is expected growth in productivity. The Intermediate projection assumes that productivity will grow at an average annual rate of 1.4 percent over the life of the forecast, which seems modest enough. But for the last twenty years, actual productivity growth has averaged only about 1 percent. That is a 40 percent difference. Without a substantial improvement in recent productivity performance, the so-called Intermediate forecasts could end up very wide of the mark, and the trust funds will be in much worse shape than currently assumed.

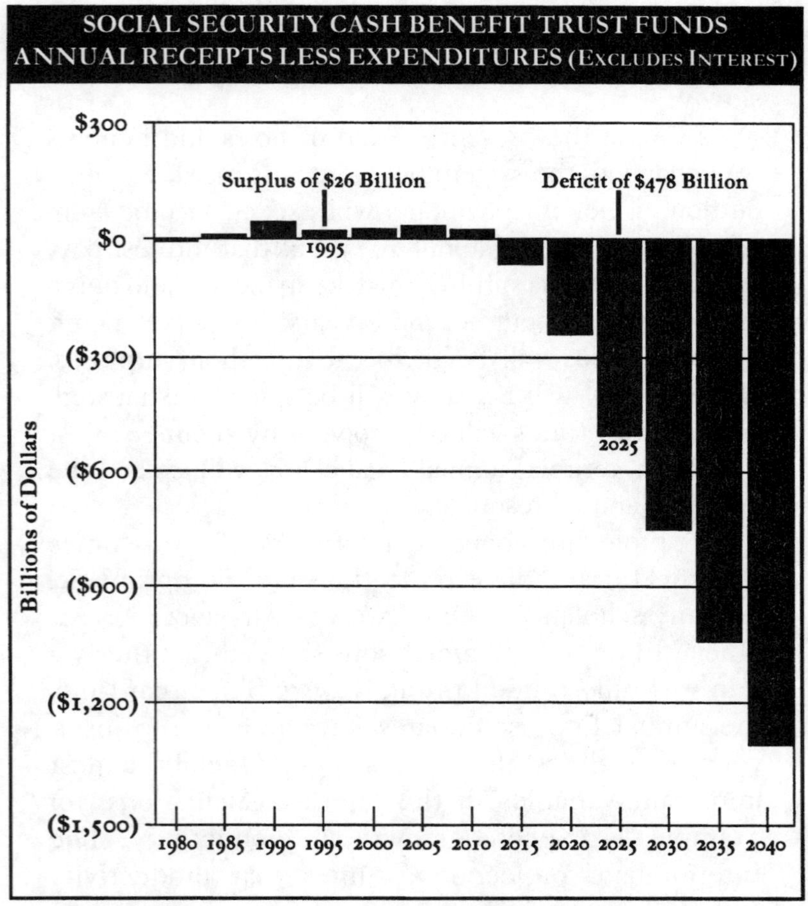


Note: Official Intermediate projection. Source: Social Security Administration, 1994.

## *The Reality of the "Surpluses"*

Another simmering question is whether the Social Security surpluses are real, or are they being siphoned off to finance the federal deficit and being replaced by "worthless IOUs." No less an authority than Senator Daniel Patrick Moynihan, one of the major architects of the 1983 reforms, seemed to say as much in 1990 when he proposed rolling back the payroll tax and returning the system to a pay-as-you-go basis. The question is a complicated one.

In the first place, from the trust funds' perspective, the surpluses are clearly not "worthless." They are invested in safe Treasury bonds and pay market interest rates. On the other hand, it is absolutely true that the surpluses have been used to finance the federal deficit despite the 1983 law that mandated that federal deficit calculations would *not* include the trust fund surpluses.

More important, if one combines the accounts of the various levels of the federal government, the surpluses vanish. One level of government, the trust funds, shows a surplus, which it has lent to another level of government, which has a corresponding debt. The surplus and the debt cancel each other out. Since the federal government is not building up a cash account to pay off the bonds when they fall due, it will have to come up with the money starting about 2019 when the trust funds start cashing in their bonds. The cash requirements to pay off the bonds will be huge, on average about $150 billion a year for ten years, in 1995 dollars. The government will have to raise the cash either through increased taxes or by borrowing, in sums that could raise interest rates and increase the cost of buying houses and cars. The cash to pay off the bonds held by the trust funds, that is, can only be raised from a new generation of workers and businesses.

In short, the trust fund surpluses are not "worthless IOUs," for there is no doubt that the government will pay them off. But it will pay them off by extracting the money, one way or the other, from the working generation of 2019–29. It is therefore misleading to think of the surpluses as a kind of government savings account that the trust funds can painlessly draw down. At the end of the day, the only source of cash for each year's required Social Security payments will always be the current generation of taxpayers.

Grim as this picture may be, it is far from a crisis. Present payroll taxes are more than enough to pay for present benefits, and by a considerable margin. Even on the government's pessimistic assumptions (the "High-Cost" as opposed to the "Intermediate" projections), there is still about twenty years to go before the trust funds will have to start spending their surpluses. Considering the Social Security system alone, and assuming that the most recent projections are not wildly off the mark, various combinations of relatively minor changes in payroll taxes, eligibility criteria, the schedule of benefit increases, and mildly skewing benefits away from people with other sources of income, would bring the system back into balance. But it is misleading to view the Social Security pension system in isolation. For it is part of a broader system of benefits, including health care. And the health care portions of the system are in much more serious trouble.

## THE PATCHWORK SYSTEM II: MEDICARE

Medicare is the federal government's national health insurance program for the aged. In general, anyone over the age of sixty-five and the long-term disabled are covered. The program is in two parts. Part A, which is automatic for all eligibles, is a hospital insurance program, covering inpatient stays and related care. It is funded by the Medicare portion of the Social Security payroll tax, which now stands at 2.9 percent, including both the employer and employee portions. A tax increase on better-off Social Security recipients, implemented in 1994, is also dedicated to finance the Part A program.

Medicare Part B is an optional insurance program available to Part A enrollees that covers physicians' services and other outpatient costs. (The official name is Supplementary Medical Insurance, or SMI.) Enrollees are charged a monthly premium for Part B coverage that is deducted directly from Social Security checks. The premium is adjusted annually, and was at $46.10 a month in 1995. Almost all Medicare-eligible enrollees elect to pay the premium.

A number of deductible and coinsurance provisions apply to both Part A and Part B coverage. For example, enrollees must pay the first $716 of the cost of a stay in the hospital, there are strict limits on nursing home care, and prescription drugs are not covered. Private insurance programs—"Medigap" policies—can be purchased to cover the most important holes in Medicare coverage. Medicare covers less than half of the health care outlays for seniors, with the remainder covered by private insurance, Medicaid, and their own resources.

The Part A, or Hospital Insurance, trust fund operates in the same way as the Social Security trust funds. Payroll taxes are paid into the fund, surpluses remaining after benefits are paid are invested in government bonds, and the fund's actuarial status is monitored in the same manner as are the Social Security funds. The Part B trust fund, on the other hand, is not an actuarial fund. Whatever payment obligations are remaining after Part B premiums are exhausted are met from general government revenues.

The Medicare program is a financial disaster area. Part A expenditures have ballooned from $5 billion in 1970 to $111.5 billion in 1995, an average annual rate of increase of more than 13 percent, or about three times the overall rate of inflation.

Absent major restructuring, the Part A trust fund will be insolvent in about five or six years, or sometime in the 2001–2002 time frame. Projections for longer periods, incorporating the retirement of the boomer generation, show almost meaninglessly large deficits. Depending on whether one uses the government's Intermediate or pessimistic estimates, Medicare payroll taxes would have to be doubled or tripled immediately—from the current 2.9 percent to a range between 5.8 and 9.1 percent—if the trust fund is to last through the peak years of the boomers' retirements. Every year the tax increases are delayed makes the eventual required increase that much bigger. To make matters worse, even more so than in the case of Social Security, many scholars doubt whether the "pessimistic" estimates are pessimistic enough. All of the government's projections, for example, forecast a substantial moderation of health care cost increases to a level no higher than increases in real wages, although there is absolutely no basis for such an assumption.

Growth in the Medicare Part B program has been even faster, from $2.2 billion in 1970 to $69 billion in 1995, for an average annual growth rate of 14.8 percent. The average monthly premium for enrollees has risen over the same period from $4 to $46.10, a somewhat slower rate of increase. Enrollee premiums will cover a bit less than 30 percent of Part B costs in 1995, with about $43.5 billion coming from general tax revenues.

Total Medicare expenditures are well on their way to overtaking the cash pension portion of the Social Security system. Medicare expenditures were only about 23 percent of Social Security outlays in 1970. By 1995, Medicare spending was about 54 percent of Social Security spending, and will rise to about 75 percent of total Social Security outlays by 2004.

## THE PATCHWORK SYSTEM III: MEDICAID

The final piece of the social insurance system for seniors is Medicaid. The aged account for only about 12 percent of Medicaid enrollees, but they incur about 31 percent of Medicaid charges. Blind and disabled people account for an additional 15 percent of recipients, and 38 percent of the charges. Put another way, although welfare recipients account for three quarters of Medicaid enrollees, they incur only about 30 percent of the charges. About six out of ten nursing home patients are financed by Medicaid. Medicaid also covers Medicare deductibles and copayments for the poor aged, and expenses like pharmaceuticals, which are not covered by Medicare.

The Medicaid program was originally intended to provide health care access for welfare recipients, on the theory that poor health was an obstacle to moving off welfare into full-time employment. (Nelson Rockefeller, who was then governor of New York, and one of the program's strongest supporters, confidently predicted that both welfare and Medicaid expenditures would *shrink* over the years as the health of welfare recipients improved.) Medicaid expenditures, in fact, have ballooned to about $155 billion in 1995, or not far short of the $183 billion tab for the Medicare program. Medicaid costs are split on a 57–43 basis overall between the federal and state governments, although the state government shares vary depending on their relative poverty. Adding the Medicare bill to the portion of Medicaid allocated to seniors brings the total government bill for senior health care to $231 billion in 1995, a number that is about two thirds the amount of cash Social Security benefits for that year. The combined Medicare/Medicaid outlay for senior health care can be expected to exceed Social Security cash payments within the next ten years.

Medicaid is means-tested, and older people are eligible only if they are poor. In the usual case, older people go onto the Medicaid rolls after they have been in a nursing home beyond the period covered by Medicare. They must then "spend down" their personal assets, until they have only $2,000 left, plus their house, furnishings, and burial plot, which usually doesn't take long. (Spouses may keep net assets of up to $75,000, including a house.) Nationwide, a month's stay in a nursing home costs about $3,000, not counting personal expenses, and in many parts of the country, monthly costs are double or triple that amount. Children, by law, are not responsible for defraying the costs of their parents' nursing care, and it is frequently disclosed that politicians or apparently well-to-do people have parents in nursing homes paid for by Medicaid. New York's governor, George Pataki, who was elected on a welfare-cutting platform, is a recent example. Even less defensible is the practice of parents and children conniving to shift assets into the children's name to achieve earlier eligibility for Medicaid. Medicaid asset-shifting is now almost an established subspecialty in American law firms.

Almost inadvertently, it seems, Medicaid has become the core program for financing America's long-term care needs. The very oldest seniors, those who are 80+ years old, are now one of the fastest-growing subpopulations in the country, and as they continue to age, large numbers will require terminal long-term nursing care. Acute health care expenditures for people eighty-five and over are twice that of people in the sixty-five- to sixty-nine-year-old bracket, and long-term care requirements are *twenty* times as high. Since the older aged are also the poorest, they are much more likely to fall back on public resources, particularly for long-term care. (An active, healthy—and still well-to-do—ninety-six-year-old commented to me: "How the hell can you plan to be ninety? I started giving all my money away when I was eighty!")

Any program to rationalize senior entitlements or to reform the American health care system that does not address the long-term care issue is like bailing a boat without plugging the gaping hole in the hull.

To date, voluntary private insurance has not been effective. Unless the insurance is purchased relatively early in life, in one's forties or fifties, premiums are crushingly high, or the payoff amounts are too low to make much difference. Most Americans in their forties and fifties are seriously undersaving for their retirements in any case; it seems too much to expect that they will, on their own initiative, start spending current income to provide for so unpleasant a prospect as a terminal nursing home bed.

Long-term care cannot be left to happenstance. The present disposition in Congress, to look steadfastly away from the looming long-term care problem, will almost certainly be productive of financial and human crises in years to come.

The next question is, how good a deal is the present system for the present generation of retirees? How good a deal will it be in the future? In short, who are the generational winners and losers?

# Chapter 5

## *Entitlement Winners and Losers: A Scorecard*

THE STEADILY RISING COSTS of social welfare provisions for the elderly have touched off, for the first time in American history, a sharp debate on "generational equity." As the investment banker Peter G. Peterson, who is one of the most vocal advocates of "entitlement reform," put it:

> In the past, entitlement reform has almost always rewarded the earlier-born at the direct expense of the later-born. But the days when we could finance entitlement windfalls to ourselves by shifting the costs to a more numerous and affluent rising generation are long gone.

Although Peterson's reform proposals are controversial, his central point is indisputable. In fact, it is part of the fundamental structure of the system. Medicare, Medicaid, and Social Security still operate primarily as pay-as-you-go systems, even taking into account recent actuarial reforms. In all three systems, moreover, benefits are calculated to rise faster than inflation. Medicare and Medicaid benefits necessarily do so, since health care costs have been rising so rapidly.

The benefit schedules of Social Security have built-in escalators both to keep pace with real wages and to ensure that the percentage of wages that are replaced by Social Security stays roughly the same from generation to generation. The escalators are built into future benefit schedules independently of the COLA provisions. It is a point worth emphasizing, since it is not widely understood. Benefits for all Social Security recipients are indexed to keep pace with inflation. But on top of the inflation indexing, benefits for each *new* cohort of retirees are indexed to keep pace with growth in real wages. That means that someone who retired in 1995, assuming growth in real wages and all else are equal, will receive a higher benefit than someone who retired in 1994.

The net effect of the increases built into the benefit system is to ensure a steady rise in the standard of living among the aged. The operation of the escalators can be seen by comparing the Social Security benefits of different generations in constant dollars—that is, correcting for the effects of inflation to show only real increases in purchasing power. A couple retiring in 1960, eligible for the middle tier or average wage-earner's benefit, would have received $9,400 in annual payments, in 1993 dollars. The same couple retiring in 1995 would receive $14,600 in 1993 dollars, a 56 percent increase in real purchasing power. Under present law, if the same hypothetical couple were to retire in 2030, they would receive $20,800 a year in 1993 dollars, or more than twice the purchasing power of the 1960 couple, and 42 percent more than the 1995 couple.

The value of the increases in health care benefits have been even larger. In just the fifteen years since 1980, the value of Medicare benefits more than doubled in constant dollar terms. Many people understandably resist thinking of medical benefits as standard-of-living improvements—far better not to be sick and not collect any benefits. But much of the recent spending increases for elderly health care is accounted for by "quality of life" medicine—angioplasties, cochlear implants, cataract surgery, arthritis medication, joint replacements. It is only fair, therefore, to count increased medical spending as a contribution to living standards.

The constant upward trend in real benefit levels underscores the nature of the generational contract: In order to finance Generation A's retirement, Generation B pays more than Generation A had to pay, because Generation A is getting an improved standard of living compared to its predecessor generation. Generation B, in turn, will expect Generation C to pay still more in order to finance yet a higher standard of living for B's retirement. Generation C, presumably, will do so uncomplainingly, because it expects the same treatment from D. But if the increases are fast enough, and projected far enough into the future, they start gobbling up more and more of national income, and the process, sooner or later, breaks down. Peterson's argument, which is based on pessimistic but not unreasonable projections, is that we are very close to reaching that point, and that it is time to restructure the contract.

## GENERATIONAL WEALTH SHIFTING

The steady rise in the real value of transfers to the aged over the past generation has resulted in a slow, but cumulatively quite remarkable, shift of wealth from working people to the elderly. In the early 1960s, for example, the spending power of the average seventy-year-old was only 71 percent that of the average thirty-year-old. By the late 1980s, however, the ratio had completely flipped. The seventy-year-old now had 18 percent *more* spending power than the thirty-year-old. On an asset basis, the comparisons are striking. According to the Census Bureau, in 1991, the median net household wealth of people over sixty-five was $88,192, most of which was in real estate. For families as a whole, however, median net household wealth was only $36,632. And the gap between seniors and the rest of the country was widening rapidly. Between 1988 and 1991, senior wealth grew by 20 percent, while median wealth for the country as a whole grew by only a bit more than 2 percent. By the early 1990s, seniors held more than half of all the net household wealth in the country, and the concentration was growing.

Seniors' money incomes are not as high as other households', but if they are adjusted to take into account other financial benefits, the money-wage differences fade away. Seniors pay lower taxes than other households—about a third as much in middle-income brackets and half as much in upper-middle-income households. Seniors, and senior advocacy organizations like AARP, of course, point out that seniors must foot much larger medical bills than nonseniors, which is true. The average out-of-pocket cost of medical care for seniors is about twice that of nonelderly households, but seniors have fewer dependents, which more than counterbalances the extra outlays for health care.

Senior housing expenses also tend to be much lower. Seniors typically purchased their houses long ago, have either paid off their mortgages or have low payments, and get property tax breaks besides. Finally, and distressingly for Mom and Dad's status as role models, it appears that seniors are much more likely to cheat on their income taxes. A detailed, if now dated, Census Bureau study showed that 37 percent of senior households underreported income, more than ten times the rate of underreporting found among nonseniors.

Average data, of course, conceal as much as they illuminate. The range of incomes among seniors is quite wide; most older black women, for instance, are still poor. More so than for any other group in the country, government transfers to seniors make the difference between financial security and poverty. Actually cutting transfers, except for those to the most well-off elderly, would have a devastating effect. But the notion that income transfers will be *cut* is a red herring. Not even the most Draconian budget hawks—not even Peterson—have proposed cutting benefits for any but the very best-off seniors.

For twenty-five years, national social policy has been consistently pro-senior, and however one teases the numbers, the effects are unmistakable. A substantial transfer of wealth from working people to seniors has created a generation of elderly that is not only the best-off elderly generation in history, which is a signal national accomplishment, but arguably the best off of any generation in the country today.

Younger people, not surprisingly, have started to notice. Advocates for children, in particular, point out that the annual cost of Social Security and Medicare for each senior is considerably more than twice what America spends to educate each of its children. And the steady rise in senior well-being is beginning to contrast uncomfortably with income stagnation among younger, lower-middle-income households, who bear the most disproportionate share of payroll taxes. Poll data consistently show that support for improved senior benefits is still quite high among younger people. But with the recent spate of publicity about alleged "greedy geezers," it would not be surprising if resistance began to grow. Recent poll data also show that a surprising number of thirty-year-olds don't expect to receive *any* Social Security benefits when they retire. Those are grossly exaggerated fears, but they may be the first windblown straws suggesting a shift in public opinion that senior advocates may ignore at their peril.

## GENERATIONAL SIZE AND DEPENDENCY

If one could freeze the senior social welfare system in place now, in 1996, one would have a system that, while expensive, would be quite sustainable. Assuming that health care cost increases could be brought down to the level of general price inflation—admittedly an enormous assumption, as we will see later—the present system looks clumsy but workable. Unfortunately, the assumptions behind the present system will be radically disrupted about fifteen years from now when the baby-boom generation starts to retire and claim their benefits.

The current growth in elder entitlement costs is occurring at a time of very slow growth of the senior population. There were about 24 million Americans over the age of seventy in 1995. That number will continue to grow slowly to 26 million by the year 2000, and to 27 million by 2010. At that point, the boomers start reaching retirement age, and the number of over-seventies explodes to 48 million in 2030.

To make the generational imbalances worse, the generation *following* the boomers is an unusually small one. Since Social Security was first enacted, the ratio of workers to retirees has been steadily dropping, mostly because older people are living so much longer. In 1950, the ratio between retirees and covered workers was 6.1 to 100—that is, the payroll taxes from 100 workers had to cover the benefit payments for 6.1 retirees. As elderly life spans increased, the ratio of retirees rose sharply to 24.3 retirees for every 100 workers in 1970. But the ratio jumps to 42.7 retirees per 100 workers in 2030. Put another way, whereas

16 covered workers supported one retiree in 1950, there will be only 2.3 covered workers to support each retiree in 2030, and the ratio will stay stuck at about that level for the next thirty years.

It is this imbalance between generations, along with the rise in health care costs, that is throwing the system into long-term crisis. It also lends perspective to notions of generational conflict. The conflict is not between *today's* workers and retirees, but, as in so many other areas of American life, between the baby boomers, who are *tomorrow's* retirees, and the generation that follows them, the hapless "Generation X," today's twentysomethings. Generation X-ers have spent their entire lives in the backwash of the disruptions strewn in the wake of the boomers' passage through American society, and that experience lends some poignancy to their expectation that they may never collect Social Security benefits. Nothing in the boomers' history suggests that they will selflessly limit their own benefits in order to preserve the system for those who follow. When 70 million boomers turn sixty-five between 2010 and 2030, they will be by far the largest and most powerful political bloc in the country and, Generation X-ers have reason to fear, may well choose to milk the system dry.

The government's official projections tell the dismal story. In 1995, the government cost of Social Security benefits and Medicare Part A and Part B was about 17 percent of covered payrolls. (The payroll tax was only 15.3 percent, because Medicare Part B is funded from general revenues, not from payroll taxes.) The official Intermediate projection has the combined cost of the three programs rising to about 22 percent of payrolls by 2010 and 34 percent of payrolls by 2030. The high-cost projections are much worse, showing cost growth to 27 percent of payrolls by 2010 and *51 percent* of payrolls in 2030. Scarily enough, however, the government's so-called high-cost projections may not be sufficiently pessimistic. Of the five major assumptions in the high-cost projections (relating to wage growth, health care costs, etc.), four of the five are *more* favorable than the experience of the past twenty years. *All* of the assumptions used in the Intermediate forecast are *more* favorable than recent actual experience. If the economy stayed on the same track it has been on for the last twenty years, and present programs were maintained unchanged, social welfare programs for the elderly would consume more than 80 percent of worker payrolls, which is, of course, absurd.

The economist Herbert Stein once remarked that unsustainable trends tend not to be sustained. Substantial modifications in senior social welfare programs are therefore inevitable. Indeed, as I will argue in chapter 9, systemic bottlenecks and other homeostatic mechanisms will kick in long before transfers rise to anywhere near the rate the official projections suggest. Even if we wanted to, that is, we couldn't spend that much on transfers. But before we look more closely at possible futures, it is useful to be more precise about who are the winners and losers from the current system.

## WHO'S GOTTEN THE BEST DEAL?

"Annuity value calculations" allow the benefit packages of one age cohort to be compared to those of another. The annuity value is the lump sum amount you would have to pay to an insurance company in return for a guaranteed lifetime stream of future benefits. Annuity values allow us to express complex future streams of benefits in terms of a single number.

In the discussion below, I will use annuity value calculations of both Medicare and Social Security benefits that were recently carried out by scholars at the Urban Institute, a Washington, D.C., think tank. The calculations assume that the current benefit package, including indexing procedures, are maintained intact. It also assumes that deficits in the trust funds will be met by raising payroll taxes. In all cases, estimates of future costs are based on the government's "Intermediate" projections. Finally, in all cases, the annuity values are expressed in 1993 dollars, so the differences from one package to the next represent real differences in purchasing power.

The annuity values clearly show the rising real value of the senior benefit package. The annuity value of the combined Social Security/Medicare package for an average-wage, one-earner couple retiring in 1970 was $250,000. If an identical couple retired in 1995, their benefits would be worth about $500,000. A similar couple retiring in 2030 would get a package worth $800,000. For a high-wage couple retiring in 2030, the annuity value of the government retirement package would be worth more than a million dollars in 1993 dollars.

The annuity value calculations can also be applied to a worker's stream of payroll tax *contributions*. That is, if you take all your lifetime payroll taxes, add them up, and assume that they were invested at a market rate of interest, you would again produce a single number, which would capture what you *paid* over your working life to qualify for government benefits. The annuity value of your lifetime tax contributions can then be compared to the annuity value of your retirement benefits to see whether or not the bargain was a good one. In fact, the annuity value of the lifetime payroll taxes paid by the average-wage, one-earner couple retiring in 1995 equates to almost precisely $250,000. But their benefit package is worth $500,000. So they have received a *net transfer* from the government of $250,000. That is to say, the benefit package that they are now entitled to receive is worth twice as much as they "earned" by their years of contributing to the system. In short, they have made a very good deal.

The table on page 102 illustrates the net transfer value of the elderly social welfare package for selected household types for three different years of retirement. Several cases are shown because the value of the benefit package, and therefore the net transfer value, varies depending on household type and earnings history. When the net transfer value is a positive number, it measures the excess value of the retirement package, compared to the beneficiaries' lifetime payroll taxes—that is, it measures how much *more* they are getting out of the system than they paid in. When it is a *negative* number, it measures how much more they paid *in* than they are getting back.

**Net Value of Retirement Package (*SS Plus Medicare*)**
**Value Received Less Taxes Paid**
**(*Constant 1993 Dollars*)**

| | Single Male | | | Two-Earner Couple | | |
|---|---|---|---|---|---|---|
| Year Retired | Low Earn. | Av. Earn. | High Earn. | Low/Low | Av./Low | High/Av. |
| **1980** | 56,500 | 61,500 | 62,200 | 165,600 | 196,300 | 204,500 |
| **1995** | 64,300 | 35,200 | -19,800 | 191,200 | 195,300 | 118,200 |
| **2030** | 88,500 | -37,200 | -351,800 | 262,200 | 175,900 | -350,600 |

Note: For the purposes of the calculation, it is assumed that the current Medicare and Social Security laws are unchanged, but that payroll taxes are raised so the trust funds are always solvent. The Intermediate cost projections are used for both Social Security and Medicare. Payroll tax contributions include both employer and employee contributions, on the theory that employer contributions operate as a deduction from salary.

The table illustrates several important points. Up until very recently, all retirees have gotten more value out of the system than they put into it. In addition, higher-earning people have gotten somewhat more value than lower-earning people. Since 1983, however, the steady increase in the maximum payroll amount subject to tax and the steady rise in the Social Security tax rate have begun to reverse the skew in favor of higher earners. As the 1995 line shows, lower-earning retirees will now generally get a better return on their taxes than their higher-earning peers. Finally, a higher-earning single male retiring in 1995 has the dubious honor of belonging to the first cohort of retirees who will actually get *less* out of the system than they put in.

In future years, the economics of the system shift much more in favor of the lower-earning retiree. The higher-earning single male and the higher-earning couple who retire in 2030—they are today's thirty-somethings—will both pay significantly more lifetime payroll taxes than they can expect to get back in benefits. With the exception of the single male, almost all average-earning retirees will also receive positive net transfers.

Annuity value calculations also help pin down whether there are any "greedy geezers" out there, and who they are. Measured as a percentage of lifetime income, net transfers to retirees clearly peaked in the early 1980s, with an especially high peak for couples—couples who are now in their middle to late seventies. Essentially, they got the full value of the rapid benefit improvements of the 1970s, but did not get stuck with the big increases in payroll taxes that were needed to bail out the system with the 1983 restructuring.

Unfortunately, anecdotal evidence suggests that *these* were the people who led the raucous—and successful—movement to repeal the Medicare Catastrophic Care Act in 1991, because it required additional premiums from wealthier seniors. That is about as good a definition of "greedy geezer" as one could ask for. (Their only excuse is that some were misinformed by inflammatory direct-mail campaigns.) It was precisely these people that Senator John McCain was citing at the Simpson hearings when he blasted AARP for being "unrepresentative."

The valuations of *future* senior social welfare packages all assume that current law will be unchanged. But current law will have to be changed, and the sooner the process begins, the better.

A sign of the times is that the leadership of AARP freely admit, at least in private, that the system will have to be modified. They are anxious that it happen in a way that is fair and orderly, and protects the most dependent elderly. But they do not dispute that the present structure of benefits is already outrunning the country's ability to pay, and guarantees a real crisis once the boomers hit the hammocks.

Part III of this book will focus on possible reform scenarios. As I said earlier, although the path to reform is a thorny one, I believe reasonable paths to a more financeable and more equitable system are open to us. But the Catastrophic Care fiasco is a warning of how daunting the politics of reform will be. The next chapter offers a brief history of the last fifteen years of reform attempts to underscore the challenges that lie ahead.

# Chapter 6

## *The Politics of Entitlements: A Report from a Fifteen-Year War*

NO REPORTER GOT THE name of the elderly lady with a sign who, on an August morning in 1989, stood in front of Congressman Dan Rostenkowski's car when he tried to leave a senior citizens' meeting in Chicago. Some reports have it that she threw herself across his hood, which would have made her an uncommonly agile old lady, but the pedestrian truth seems to be that she just stood there. But whether she jumped or stood, her action was one of those small events, the little rocks in the stream, that mark a perceptible shift in the direction of the great river of American politics.

Rostenkowski was chairman of the House Ways and Means Committee, one of the most powerful politicians in America, a longtime advocate for the aged, meeting with senior citizens in the friendly confines of his own district, and here he was being roundly heckled and booed, "peeling old folks off the hood of my car," as he rather dramatically put it, and forced to retreat from the meeting on foot. To make matters more unsettling, the protests were over the Medicare

Catastrophic Coverage Act, which Congress had proudly passed only the year before, hailing it as the first major extension of the Medicare program since its inception.

The old people "shook more than Rosty's car," said Washington-based political analyst Kevin Phillips. "They shook the willingness of politicians to confront retirees." The tremors were even felt at the foundations of AARP itself. In the summer of 1989, busloads of old people picketed AARP's Florida headquarters in St. Petersburg carrying "Down With AARP!" signs because the organization supported the Medicare Catastrophic Care Act. The spectacle of elderly citizens demonstrating outside AARP offices was repeated throughout the country. Congressmen and senators reported receiving thousands of angry letters from elderly voters every day.

The reaction in Washington was panicky flight. In October, the House voted 360–66 for outright repeal of an act they had passed overwhelmingly just the year before. The Senate held out stubbornly for another six weeks in favor of a patch-up plan sponsored by Senator McCain, but finally caved in and went along with the House. President Bush had long made it clear that he would sign any bill the Congress passed. The White House hasn't "even been involved enough to be ambivalent," one congressman commented waspishly. No one can remember when another major piece of legislation was passed by a large margin one year only to be repealed by an even bigger margin the next. In the House, 328 congressmen who had voted for the Catastrophic Act in 1988, including some of the Act's sponsors, switched their vote and backed repeal in 1989.

The Catastrophic Coverage Act had its genesis in a modest initiative from Ronald Reagan's secretary of Health and Human Services, Otis Bowen, a conservative midwestern Republican. It was, arguably, the only social welfare initiative of the entire Reagan presidency. Bowen lost his wife to a long bout with cancer in 1985, just before he joined the cabinet. Unlike some other cabinet members, he was not a wealthy man, and had learned firsthand that Medicare coverage runs out after sixty continuous days in the hospital. Many seniors had Medigap insurance to patch over Medicare's shortcomings, but these were the days before Medigap coverage had been standardized, and the coverage of many policies ranged from the inadequate to the outright fraudulent. In truth, continuous hospital stays of more than sixty days are rare, and Bowen calculated that the hospital limit could be extended substantially at a very small increase in cost. Paying for the additional days through Medicare would also be much cheaper than relying on Medigap policies, because of their high sales and marketing costs. He therefore proposed, and Reagan approved, a modest extension of Medicare coverage that would be financed by an increase of $4.92 a month in Medicare Part B payments, a 27 percent hike. It was enough to be noticeable but not really onerous, and almost all seniors would have come out ahead. Those who already had Medigap coverage would have dropped it, or could have bought narrower coverage at lower premiums.

The proposal was formally sent to Congress in early 1987; rarely was a Reagan proposal ever met with such enthusiasm. Claude Pepper, the octogenarian Floridian who chaired the House Committee on Aging, and who had spent his career leading the charge for more benefits for seniors, immediately began dressing up Bowen's modest proposal with benefits that seniors had wanted for years, like nursing home coverage, home care (including live-in maids for the disabled elderly), and prescription drugs. AARP and other senior advocates joined in the fun, and although Pepper's wilder excrescences were eventually pruned away, the final bill constituted a major improvement in Medicare coverage, including some benefits, like long-term care and prescription drugs, that the senior lobby had yearned after for years. (AARP did some soul-searching before backing the program, because it would have put a crimp in their lucrative Medigap business, but they decided the government package was truly a better deal for seniors.)

The problem was how to pay for it. Under the Gramm-Rudman deficit reduction rules then in effect, every new spending initiative had to be packaged with its own revenue proposal. AARP tried holding out for a general tax increase, but there was no way that could pass muster at the Reagan White House. Over AARP's objections, the leadership decided that seniors would have to pay for the package themselves, as Bowen had originally proposed. AARP and other advocacy organizations grudgingly went along, because the benefits were so attractive, and because the Medicare funding mechanism was much more cost-effective than the Medigap alternative. Lower-income seniors, however, were not likely to see it that way, because many of them didn't buy Medigap coverage, and the full Catastrophic Care premium increase would look very steep. (In the argot of advocacy, a premium increase is a benefit cut, and congressmen hate cutting benefits.)

The solution was to have a two-tier premium structure. The average senior would pay an increase of only $4 a month. The rest would be made up by a surtax on the "affluent" aged, defined as anyone in the income brackets where their Social Security became taxable. Seniors who paid at least $150 in income taxes had a 15 percent surtax added to their bill. The surtax was capped at $800 the first year, rising to $1,050 in 1993. In the first year under the new legislation, about 44 percent of all seniors would have had to pay some surtax, but only the 6 percent or so with incomes over $50,000 would have had to pay the full $800. Senator Simpson called it "a social experiment. It's called pay for what you get, especially if you've got the wherewithal to do it." AARP told their members that the plan wasn't everything they had hoped for, but was a good deal nonetheless.

Congressmen began to report rumblings among their constituents during the 1988 fall recess. But the rumblings turned into a roar when the premium increases took effect in the new year, and better-off seniors began to hear from their tax accountants. A host of direct-mail fund-raising organizations sprang up spreading fear and loathing of the "seniors-only surtax." The most notorious was the National Committee to Preserve Social Security and Medicare, headed by James Roosevelt, a former congressman and a son of the former president. Most, like the United Seniors of America and the Conservative Caucus, urged seniors to make cash contributions to "help save millions of Americans (including you) from paying an extra $800 per year (and more) in taxes—year after year after year." Officials of the Roosevelt organization later conceded that they may have misled people into believing that all seniors would have to pay the $800 maximum surtax. The usually mild Deets still shows a flush of anger when he talks about organizations that spread fear to solicit money. (The National Committee, under Martha McSteen, a former Social Security official, has greatly improved its reputation in recent years.)

To its credit, AARP was the only seniors' advocacy organization that refused to back repeal. All other organizations, like most congressmen, ran for cover. The simple fact was that AARP's analyses, like those of the Congressional Budget Office, showed that some two thirds of seniors were better off with the Catastrophic Coverage legislation. The main "losers" were the 3.3 million retirees whose previous employers provided free Medigap-type coverage—they typically also had private pensions, and could expect to pay some surtax as well. As they saw it, they were "paying twice for the same benefit, or paying for benefits they don't want or need." In addition, taken by itself, the new package was not a good deal for people in the top surtax brackets. The combined Part B premium increase and the surtax was usually more than they had to pay for Medigap coverage, although the difference was on the order of a few hundred dollars per year in most cases.

To talk about "losers," of course, is almost ludicrous in the context of the total Social Security/Medicare package. As we saw in the last chapter, people who were in their seventies in 1989 got government benefits worth several times their and their employers' Social Security tax contribution, and upper-income people got one of the very best deals of all. At worst, the Catastrophic Coverage surtax was a minimal readjustment in an extremely generous transfer program. But all of the anecdotal reports suggest that it was primarily the relatively affluent seniors who took to the barricades, disowned AARP, pounded on Rostenkowski's car, and sent the Congress into a headlong, squealing flight.

The epistemology of the Catastrophic Care fiasco is still being sorted out. AARP's legislative director, John Rother, prefers to concentrate on "the power of the negative message." Complicated good things are tough to sell against simplistic negative slogans, however inaccurate. The implicit assumption is that seniors would have supported Catastrophic Coverage had they been properly informed. Deets says, "We did seven pieces in the *AARP Bulletin* on Catastrophic Coverage, and we thought that was communication. It wasn't nearly enough." The bruising experience with Catastrophic Coverage is behind the long-term AARP program to decentralize its operations to get closer to its grass roots.

A less optimistic interpretation is that there really are "greedy geezers" out there. One not-untypical senior quote was that farmers "aren't the only ones to pay for farm subsidies"—in effect, Simpson's new principle of "pay for what you get" be damned. (My own extremely unscientific, and very limited, straw poll of AARP chapter members—a fairly affluent sample—didn't turn up anyone who had been in favor of Catastrophic Coverage, although everyone seemed to understand it. One or two, at least, were a little embarrassed—"Maybe we *are* greedy geezers" was one comment.) The episode also lends substance to the fears of many liberals that wealthier people will push through the right to opt out of the Social Security system if benefits are ever means-tested. Notions of intragenerational solidarity—of the communitarian help-each-other variety—may be naive, at least on a large scale.

For congressmen, the legacy of Catastrophic Coverage is a toxic trail of anger and fear. Fear of the formidable power wielded by aroused seniors. Anger at the irresponsible lobbying campaigns that scuttled the Act. Anger at their own cravenness in not standing up for what most probably still believe was a good piece of legislation.

The episode has also had a profound, if subtle, effect on the position of AARP in Washington politics. It is still the most prestigious and respected seniors' advocacy organization, but it can no longer claim to be quite the voice of seniors that it once was. As a longtime congressional aide put it: "The AARP lobbyists are still very credible . . . but while there once would have been a willingness to accept whatever AARP said about an issue, now everybody checks everything three times from Sunday." AARP's congressional lobbyist, Martin Corry, doesn't dispute the point: "Congressmen still listen," he says, "but they are much more likely to check what we say against what they hear from their own grass roots. If our message doesn't jibe with what in their gut they think they hear from home—even when they agree with us—they will discount it or shut it out."

But the changed position of AARP, or the shaken congressional self-confidence, may be among the more minor effects of the Catastrophic Care fiasco. In a broader context, it is only the most dramatic recent example of deeper changes in American politics that will profoundly affect the eventual working through of the entitlements issue.

## THE POLITICS OF SOCIAL SECURITY

In early January of 1983, just as Congress was reconvening after the holiday break, a small group of congressional leaders from both parties—Pat Moynihan, Dan Rostenkowski, Pete Domenici, Barber Conable, Bob Dole, Howard Baker—quietly got together in a town house near Washington's Lafayette Park. Richard Darman, the White House's legislative strategist, was invited, as was Alan Greenspan, then a private economic forecaster. The meeting was called because the Social Security trust fund was careening toward bankruptcy—all the money would be gone before the end of the year. (But no one thought for a minute that the checks might actually stop.)

Greenspan was there because he had been asked to head a presidential commission to recommend a rescue plan.

Greenspan's commission had met through the fall of 1982, but had not come close to a consensus. The problem was that the schedule of benefits that Congress and the Nixon administration had put into effect in the 1970s, partly because of simple calculation errors, was far richer than Social Security tax revenues could support. The deficits had now grown too big to be patched over. To make matters worse, in the first heady months of the Reagan administration, the new budget director, David Stockman, an antispending ideologue, had made a futile run at cutting Social Security benefits. The Senate, led by Moynihan, passed a unanimous resolution (96–0) disowning Stockman's plan, but Republicans were tarred by the Stockman initiative and had been mauled in the 1982 congressional elections. Their polls suggested that Stockman's foolhardy riling of seniors had cost them twenty-five to thirty seats. No one, understandably, had any appetite for playing the role of Social Security hatchetman.

But everybody at the Lafayette Park meeting knew that there was no more room for playing politics as usual. They came to the meeting ready to do business, and at the end of the day shook hands on a solution that involved real benefit cuts and very substantial tax increases. Reagan blessed the package a day or two later, and Greenspan quietly had it baptized by his commission, so it could be announced as a commission plan. Passage through Congress was by no means an assured thing, since all the powerful seniors' advocacy organizations, including AARP, denounced almost every feature of the plan. The National Council of Senior Citizens was "adamantly opposed," while AARP and several other organizations vowed to fight an "all-out, grassroots campaign" to defeat it. But the leadership kept their coalitions together—the Greenspan Commission was a convenient flak-catcher—and the package passed by comfortable margins (243–102 in the House; 58–14 in the Senate). President Reagan hailed the legislation as a way to "allow Social Security to age as gracefully as all of us hope to do ourselves," and the so-called Greenspan plan governs the system still.

The 1983 Social Security restructuring was a signal demonstration of the ability of skilled political professionals to strike a bargain and stick to it. And it may be the last time that has happened in Washington.

The episode also prompted some serious self-assessments at AARP. Through most of its history, the AARP political line was notably shrill. "Not since World War II has the well-being of older Americans been in more danger than it is in 1982" was a fairly typical sample of the editorial style of *Modern Maturity*. But for all of its vaunted power as the eight-hundred-pound gorilla of modern lobbying, AARP was simply brushed aside during the restructuring debate. Rother was brought in in late 1983—he had been staff director for the Senate Committee on Aging—to win, as he puts it, a seat at the table for AARP and to develop more nuanced positions on aging issues. The old AARP was "pretty strident," Rother concedes, but he says, "Power brings responsibility. . . . You just can't take extreme positions when you're this big. You must accept your share of the sacrifice."

### *The Senate Walks the Plank*

Even with the Social Security crisis out of the way, the Reagan administration's fiscal policy was still in chaos. Reagan had come into office loudly denouncing budget deficits in the low tens of billions. In his first two years, he had engineered massive tax cuts and massive increases in defense spending but had failed to make any serious cuts in social programs. The government was now staring at $200+ billion deficits "as far as the eye can see," as Stockman put it.

With the 1984 elections behind them, and the Democrats in shock from the scale of the Reagan landslide, the Senate Republican leadership, led by Dole and Domenici, began to cobble together another "grand compromise" comprising substantial budget cuts combined with tax increases to put the administration's fiscal house back in some semblance of order. Through the winter and early spring, the Republican senators came up with $54 billion in budget cuts, roughly split between defense and social programs, and including a freeze in Social Security COLAs. The showdown vote came in May 1985, and the leadership won, but only by dint of then-senator Pete Wilson of California, who was recovering from surgery, being hustled onto the Senate floor strapped to a hospital gurney to cast a tie vote. Vice President George Bush broke the tie and carried the package.

The deal collapsed in the House. Corry's recollection

is that "it just took too long. By the time it got to the House, the Democrats had recovered their voices." The public story was that Tip O'Neill cut a deal with Reagan, but the defeat in the House was actually engineered by Republicans. The legend is that now-senator Trent Lott and Jack Kemp made an alarmed visit to the White House and begged Reagan to take Social Security off the table, conjuring up the ghost of the 1982 fall elections. When Reagan agreed, the Senate leaders felt betrayed. They had walked the plank, with the administration's encouragement, only to have Reagan saw it away behind them.

The 1985 debacle was a watershed in Social Security politics. From that point, in Moynihan's words, Social Security was "off the table," and mucking with COLAs, he later warned the Clinton administration, was a "death wish." The Gramm-Rudman deficit-reduction act, passed immediately in the wake of the Social Security disaster, was an explicit self-acknowledgment of Congress's failure. Unable to address the fiscal chaos directly, they fell back on process rules that, it was well understood, could be easily waived whenever they became inconvenient.

The accession of new Republican majorities in the wake of the 1994 congressional elections confirms the essential correctness of Moynihan's 1985 statement. Despite the fulminations of senators like Kerrey, Simpson, and Danforth that Social Security is headed for another crisis when the boomers start to retire, the official line, in the words of House Speaker Newt Gingrich, is that the budget can be balanced "without touching" Social Security—in effect, the program is still off the table.

## THE NEW POLITICS OF MEDICARE

"It's truly amazing how the political salience of Medicare has grown," AARP's Corry says. "Medicare's been on the table every year, but it's really only this year [1995] that it's moved into the same league as Social Security. All of our research shows that people see Medicare as an income security issue, not primarily as a health care issue. Paying for health care is now a major pocketbook issue. And with so much corporate downsizing and early retirements, there are a lot of people in their fifties paying thousands of dollars out-of-pocket each year for health insurance, just hoping that they can hang on until their Medicare kicks in."

The center-stage attention to Medicare, of course, is driven primarily by the growth in costs. Congress is reaching the limits of the strategy of curtailing Medicare costs by focusing on providers rather than beneficiaries. Since 1983, as AARP is fond of pointing out, there have been $600 billion in "cuts" in Medicare. (Senator Simpson goes ballistic at the use of the word *cut* in this context, because total costs have continued to grow rapidly. A rise in Part B premiums, of course, looks like a "cut" to a recipient, even if it doesn't offset total cost growth. *Curtailments* may be a better word.) But only about a quarter of the recent curtailments have fallen directly on recipients. The rest have been borne by providers—the hospital and physician flat-payment systems inaugurated in the 1980s are the most dramatic examples. One of the great advantages of this strategy from a political perspective was that cost-reduction initiatives were played out in the form of highly technical discussions between experts. Reimbursement arcana are not the stuff of mass political movements.

There is now substantial evidence, however, that Medicare provider payment curtailments have rapidly translated into increased charges to non-Medicare patients. In effect, they are a hidden payroll tax. Much of the recent provider "cuts" may not have been cuts at all, but simply silent tax increases on workers and businesses. In any case, it seems clear that future program curtailments will fall much more directly on beneficiaries than they have to date.

### *The Bush-Darman 1990 Deficit Package*

Medicare costs arguably first became a political issue in their own right only with the 1990 Bush-Darman deficit reduction package. George Bush, it may be recalled, had won office on his famous "Read my lips. No new taxes" pledge. It is not clear whether he ever meant it; certainly his budget director, Richard Darman, didn't. His second year in office, to the dismay of party professionals, Bush called a bipartisan summit conference at Andrews Air Force Base to put together a major deficit reduction program, including tax increases, spending cuts, and sharp increases in Medicare copayments and deductibles. It was understood from the outset, in Bush's words, that the deficit-cutting negotiations would not "mess with Social Security."

The package that emerged from the Andrews meeting had no fathers. Republicans hated the tax increases. Democrats hated the spending cuts. According to Corry, although AARP participated in ritual denunciations of the cuts for seniors, they did not activate their grassroots networks, because they expected the package to melt down of its own accord, as it promptly proceeded to do.

After the Bush-Darman package was quickly disowned by all concerned, a much more modest package was eventually hammered out in the Congress. The Medicare cuts were reduced to $44 billion, with only $10 billion charged directly to seniors. To further sweeten the pill, the final 1990 legislation also included some minor, but long-sought expansions of Medicare—to cover mammographies, for instance—and a softening of Medicaid eligibility rules to ensure that some of the increased premiums for poorer seniors would be picked up by the government. An important nonfiscal add-on was legislation creating nationwide standards for Medigap insurance.

AARP was a participant in the final negotiation and supported the bill. "When we decide to support a bill," says Corry, "we sign on to the team. We believe you have to be prepared to do that. In this case, we helped work the floor and were on call to help out if a waverer needed more information to bolster a yes vote."

### *The 1993 Clinton Deficit Package*

Bill Clinton's 1993 deficit reduction package once again made Medicare the center of attention, although Social Security did not escape unscathed. The White House floated a trial balloon about cutting COLAs, which was almost instantly shot down in flames, but a tax increase on better-off Social Security recipients slipped through with remarkably little comment, because it was dedicated to the Medicare trust fund. By treating the Social Security tax increase as a Medicare funding device, rather than as a change in Social Security, rhetorically at least, Social Security was still off the table.

The jockeying over the Medicare cuts was particularly fierce, even though virtually none of them applied directly to beneficiaries. Out of a final package of $56 billion worth of projected curtailments over a five-year period, only about $1 billion came out of recipients' pockets; and that was merely from tightening the rules by which beneficiaries could become eligible for Medicaid by shifting assets to their children.

The heat was generated more by process than content. Early on, Clinton had made a special appeal to AARP and other senior lobbying organizations, and Rostenkowski leaned on AARP to "help this young man." The agreement that AARP signed onto included substantial Medicare cuts—virtually all of them coming from hospital and physician reimbursement, however—and a complicated energy tax. The package squeaked by the House more or less intact, but got bogged down in the Senate Finance Committee because of objections by senators from energy-producing states. To AARP's outrage, Clinton quickly caved in on a Senate proposal to substitute more Medicare cuts for the energy tax.

After a nasty backstairs fight that raged from the Finance Committee to the Senate floor and finally to the House-Senate conference committee, most, but by no means all, of the additional Medicare curtailments were rescinded. There was, in any case, an air of unreality about the reductions in hospital and physician payments because most of the participants in the debate, especially the White House, confidently expected to take a fresh look at provider reimbursement as part of the national health care reform bill, the next big item on the Clinton agenda.

The AARP board did not support the proposal—the first time they had not supported a deficit reduction bill since 1982. "Supporting it was out of the question," says Corry. The tax provisions were a problem to begin with, but their treatment by the White House was decisive. It is clear that AARP could have defeated the bill if it had chosen to do so; it passed the Senate only by dint of Vice President Al Gore's tie-breaking vote. Instead, AARP chose to sit on its hands, in part because of its long-standing commitment to deficit reduction, but also so as not to poison the waters for the upcoming health care debate.

## *The New Republican Agenda*

After the failure of Clinton's health care reform legislation in 1993, and the return of Republican majorities in the 1994 congressional elections, senior health care once again moved to the top of the policy agenda. As this book goes to press in the winter of 1996, the Republican majorities have agreed on a seven-year budget-balancing and tax-cutting agenda that will require lowering the projected rate of increase in Medicare spending by about a fourth, from 10 percent a year to 7.5 percent a year, for a total saving over the period of $270 billion, and an additional $182 billion from Medicaid.

It bears repeating, as Simpson and others insist, that the *rate of spending increase* in Medicare will be cut, but *total spending* will continue to rise rapidly. It is, however, *also* true, as Deets insists with equal fervor, that *overall benefit packages* will have to be cut in order to achieve the projected level of savings. The Republican package gradually emerging is the usual mix of heavy cuts in provider reimbursements, which will simply generate more cost-shifting to the private sector—in other words, a hidden payroll tax—and a stiff increase in beneficiary Part B premiums.

House Speaker Newt Gingrich once hoped to save large amounts of money by transforming Medicare into a "managed care" program (setting up HMOs, or health maintenance organizations, for seniors), but those hopes seem to have been quietly dropped. As we will see in the next chapter, while managed care may generate some savings, and possibly even improve care, the savings won't be on the scale Gingrich seemed to hope for. There are, in fact, substantial savings slated for HMOs, but they mostly come from cutting managed care *fees*, not from increasing efficiency. The final package will probably also include a modest privatizing initiative—giving seniors the right to buy low-cost catastrophic insurance, while assuming the risk for normal health expenditures, and banking the difference in tax-free "health savings accounts." It is not likely there will be many takers, since the concept makes much more sense for young people.

Suffice it to say, for all the trial balloons and the

hoopla over radical reform, the Republican program had withered down to essentially the same tried-and-true remedies of the previous twelve years, only a bit more of them.

More worrisome in its implications for seniors is the proposal to reconstitute Medicaid as a "block grant" program administered by the states, while freezing federal spending amounts. Medicaid, as we have seen, is now the primary source of funding for long-term care for the aged, and Democratic analysts estimate that the Republican proposals will equate to a 30 percent federal Medicaid spending cut by 2002.

Certainly, once detailed spending decisions are pushed down to the state level, pro-Medicaid lobbyists will face a much more diffuse target. The history of federal manpower training and community development programs is instructive: After they were transformed into block grants, they were steadily reduced and in a few cases actually eliminated. Medicaid's image as "welfare" medicine—its role in nursing home funding is not widely appreciated—also makes it much easier to attack than Medicare. Over the longer term, a block grant status for Medicaid will merely increase the urgency of making some more rational provision for long-term care.

With presidential elections looming in 1996, the Republican majority is displaying a dawning awareness that it is swimming against the tide of public opinion. Poll after poll shows that a very strong majority of Americans are in favor of balanced budgets and tax cuts. But even *stronger* majorities, by a remarkable three or four to one, oppose cutting Social Security and Medicare, *even if* it means forgoing tax reduction or budget balancing. Both Senate Majority Leader Bob Dole and Speaker Gingrich insist that they are attempting to "save Medicare," not cut it. If the Worcester meeting described in chapter 3 is any indication, that will be a tough sell. The Republican task will not be made any easier by the fact that key Republicans, and some of the loudest voices in favor of balanced budgets, like Senators Lott and McCain and Congressmen Bill Archer and Dick Armey, have *also* been among the most obstinate in opposing cost-sharing even for the better-off elderly, as in Catastrophic Care or the 1993 Social Security tax increase—or, in the case of McCain, even supporting the fiscally irresponsible "Notch Repair" initiative in 1992.

Adding to the Republican sales problem is that their proposed tax cuts, which, like those for taxes on capital gains, tend to benefit the better-off, are suspiciously close to their proposals for Medicare savings ($245 billion in tax cuts and $270 billion in Medicare savings). Kicking seniors out of nursing homes to put more after-tax dollars in the pockets of the Gucci loafer and Rolex watch crowd is not a pretty picture, and Republicans risk setting themselves up for a 1996 presidential campaign against a Bill Clinton draped in the mantle of defender of senior benefits against the piratical rich. In the Senate, at least, the tax-cut fervor seems distinctly to have waned. There are even some signs that Social Security may be put back *on* the table. Senator Moynihan has pointed out that small revisions in the Consumer Price Index—many economists think it overstates inflation—would save hundreds of billions in scheduled Social Security payments over the next decade, and also generate substantial savings in other "indexed" federal programs.

Recognizing the hazards of matching book publication schedules to political developments, as of early 1996, it is a good bet that some form of the Republican program will pass, probably after substantial rollbacks in both tax cuts and program cuts—and probably after dramatic confrontations with the White House, a veto threat, and some passing hysteria about budget gridlock bringing the entire federal machinery to a halt. In the final analysis, growth in benefits will have temporarily slowed, Medicare insolvency will have been postponed a few more years, and the problem of what to do when the boomers begin to retire will still loom like a fiscal Mount Everest.

In the next section, we will elevate our viewing angle above the current political fray and look at the actual limits and the opportunities of longer-term reform.

# III

# *The Transformation of American Society*

# Chapter 7

# *The Realities of Reform*

ALTHOUGH THERE IS A strong case for regarding Social Security and Medicare as components of a single elderly social insurance program, they are separately funded and face problems that are of quite different scale and complexity.

## FIXING SOCIAL SECURITY

### *Reform Alternatives*

It cannot be too often repeated that, *considered by itself*, Social Security is fundamentally a sound system that is *not* in crisis. The 1983 restructuring took a long-term view and imposed tax increases and benefit modifications that were sufficiently Draconian to put the program on a sound actuarial basis according to the then-current projections. Those projections have turned out to be too optimistic, and without further modifications, the system will begin running operating deficits about fifteen years from now, and will become insolvent in thirty to thirty-five years. But insolvency is clearly not imminent. If fairly modest reforms were instituted now, actuarial integrity could be restored without undue pain.

A reform package could meet current actuarial tests with some combination of the following measures:

- A slowdown in COLA growth by perhaps 0.5 percent. (The current inflation standard, the Consumer Price Index, may actually overstate inflation by at least that amount.)
- A payroll tax increase of about 1 percent, for both employers and employees.
- A gradual reduction of the current schedule of growth in initial benefits, on the order of 10 to 15 percent, with the reductions skewed to the higher earners. Benefit levels would still rise for all, or almost all, recipients, but the increases would be at a lower rate. Depending on the schedules adopted, benefit growth for wealthier recipients would probably be much flatter than it is now.
- Relatively small increases in taxes on benefits, on a sliding scale to protect the elderly poor.
- A gradual increase in the normal retirement age to seventy, or an acceleration of the increase in the normal age to sixty-seven that has already been scheduled. Arguably the average seventy-year-old is now as healthy and as able to support himself as a sixty-five-year-old was in 1940.

It is important to note that *no* recipient's benefits need actually be cut to achieve long-term solvency. Beneficiaries would see, at worst, a flattening out of the curve of improvement. The schedule of future increases for lower-income beneficiaries need hardly change at all. The modification alternatives described above are interacting—that is, slightly higher payroll taxes could be exchanged for somewhat lower benefit curtailments and vice versa.

The net effect of the most likely changes would be to substantially reduce the net transfers to average- and high-wage earners. It is likely that a postreform computation of lifetime Social Security payroll taxes versus lifetime Social Security benefits would show average-earner recipients roughly breaking even, or at best slightly better, while higher earners would put more into the system over their working lives than they would take out. Given the long-standing American commitment to a mildly progressive tax system, that does not seem to be an unreasonable result.

While it is accurate to say that Social Security is not in crisis, the more time that is wasted implementing reforms, the more expensive and the more onerous they will become. The current political penchant on both sides of the aisle to keep Social Security "off the table" will only make reform more difficult than it needs to be. I will return to this issue in chapter 9.

## *The Question of the "Surpluses"*

As detailed in chapter 4, the large surpluses purportedly being earned by the trust funds are extremely misleading. An honest and accurate presentation of the true character of the surpluses is a prerequisite for meaningful reforms. Good intentions to the contrary, they are *not* real surpluses, and have allowed the federal government to defer difficult spending and budget-cutting decisions. The problem may be summarized as follows:

- Since the payroll tax surpluses are lumped in with general revenues, they *do* mask the scale of federal deficit spending—on all programs, not just entitlements.

- When the surpluses are invested in Treasury bonds, they are being borrowed to finance the deficit—that is, the surpluses, which are an asset of the trust funds, become a liability of the federal government. The asset of one level of government is canceled out by the liability of the other. The net effect is zero.

- The surpluses are not "worthless IOUs," because the federal government will pay them back. But in order to do so, it will have to raise new funds by taxing or borrowing. It is therefore misleading to say that the trust funds can "draw on their accumulated surpluses." When the trust funds need their money, the federal government will have to go to the taxpayer to get it.

- When the trust funds begin calling in the government's IOUs at an annual average clip of $150 billion+ fifteen to twenty years from now, the government will have to scramble to raise the cash from that generation of workers and taxpayers. That is not what most people would understand as a "surplus."

One plausible solution to the problem of the surpluses, recently suggested by Senator Bob Kerrey among others, is to invest a substantial portion of the surpluses—Kerrey has suggested half—in private financial instruments. There are readily available investing techniques to avoid favoritism and financial disruption. Kerrey's suggestion would increase liquidity in the private markets, would possibly improve trust fund returns, and would improve the accuracy of federal deficit reporting. A second alternative would be to revive Senator Moynihan's proposal to cut the payroll tax and return to a "pay-as-you-go" system, rather than perpetrate fictions about "surpluses."

Realistically, the private investment option has little chance of becoming law, and the Moynihan proposal has been roundly denounced by both parties. A simpler change, which would have the advantage of showing the true costs of social insurance, would be to consolidate the reporting of the Medicare and Social Security trust funds and shift the financing of Medicare Part B to the combined trust funds. Since the government's Part B contribution currently exceeds the surplus Social Security payroll tax collections, the apparent surpluses would disappear, and the true costs and actuarial status of the social insurance program would be much more clearly visible.

## CONTROLLING HEALTH CARE SPENDING

At the end of the day, entitlement reform is about health care, for it is primarily ballooning health care expenditures that are driving the growth in senior social insurance spending. No spending reform can be effective that does not restrain health care spending, but coming up with a plausible program of health care reform presents challenges of exquisite difficulty.

### *The Reality Behind the Spending*

There is much that is wrong with the American health care system. It is the most expensive in the world by a very large margin. It is the most paperwork-intensive and the hardest for the unsophisticated to negotiate. The gap between the care available to the better-off and to the poor is among the widest anywhere, and the holes in the insurance system gape the broadest. The system is litigious and burdened with flocks of malpractice lawyers ready to pounce on any misstep, or even any unfortunate outcome. The addiction to high-tech solutions, sometimes in defiance of common sense, is the most engrained in the world.

But the American health care system also provides higher-quality care to more people than any other system in the world. There is a vogue for extolling foreign systems, like the government-run system in Canada. But Canada keeps a much tighter rein on expensive treatments than America does. In Canada, for example, there are strict limits on the number of dialysis machines in each province; in the United States, Congress has *mandated* that Medicare pay for all end-stage renal-disease treatment, which has encouraged the proliferation of dialysis machines, including home machines, and has prolonged many worthy lives, including those of many younger people, at an annual cost of $6 billion. Is it worth it? How do you tell?

If an older Canadian cardiac patient has chest pains and shortness of breath, he learns to live, and die, with chest pains and shortness of breath. A researcher who has studied both systems told me that in America, "the patient *tells the doctor*, 'Let's start with an angioplasty, and if that doesn't work, we'll go for the bypass.'" American cultural attitudes—the tendency to be highly demanding consumers, to insist on every jot and tittle of one's rights—clearly play a role. AARP's Rother points out that the cost differences among U.S. regions—say, between high-demand areas like New York City and south Florida and smaller cities in the Midwest and West—are greater than the average cost differences between America and Canada. In any case, Canada's health care costs are now closing in on 10 percent of GDP, and are growing faster than in America.

Detailed international comparisons have shown that America has the highest concentration of high-technology medicine. In one recent survey, the United States had 7.4 times as many radiation therapy units per capita and eight times the MRI units as Canada; 4.4 times as many open-heart surgery units and 2.4 times as many lithotripsy units as West Germany (lithotripsy is a technique for the nonsurgical breakup of kidney stones). The examples could be multiplied—organ transplants, heart implants, cochlear implants (hearing), microsurgeries—these are all life-saving and life-enhancing therapies that American health care consumers know about and demand from their doctors.

Superficially, American hospital costs look much higher than in other industrialized countries. But more goes on in American hospitals. Patients are rotated in and out much faster, so there is a much higher concentration on the most acute stages of caregiving and a much higher intensity of high-technology services. Daniel Patrick Moynihan points to the sharp jump in the life spans of the elderly, and says, "The reason American health care costs so much is that it *works*. We're paying the price of success! And it's very expensive."

It is frequently alleged that standard health indicators, such as average life span and infant mortality rates, suggest that American health care is actually very poor. But such generic measures are at most indirectly related to medical care. High youthful death rates from violence and AIDS, for example, drag down mortality statistics, while the lack of prenatal care among poorer women is responsible for most of the lag in infant mortality. The statistics are more a reflection of American social conditions, and in some cases the quality of *access* to health care, than of the quality of care itself.

Detailed studies of the cost structure of American health care refute the easy notion that costs are driven by "waste and fraud." Even the most aggressive estimates suggest that only about 5 to 8 percent of total spending results from outright fraud. One careful study made maximum plausible estimates of the savings that would accrue by eliminating excessive paperwork, defensive medicine, duplicate services, physician-owned diagnostic centers (that are claimed to increase testing rates), and excess hospital beds—all the most frequently cited causes of excess costs. The conclusion was that health care cost growth would slow from 6.5 percent a year to 5 percent a year, a rate that is still much faster than inflation. A 1.5 percent per year average cost reduction—this is a *maximum* assumption—is not to be sneezed at, but it does not get at the heart of the problem. Medicare spending increases are at a much higher rate, recently at an annual average of about 10 percent.

Costs are driven, at bottom, by improvements in care. A decade or so ago, many types of diagnoses required exploratory surgery or other highly invasive techniques, which were both dangerous and expensive. A revolution in noninvasive diagnostics, like MRI and PET scanning, has greatly lowered the costs and risks of individual diagnoses and vastly improved diagnostic accuracy. But precisely because they are such splendid advances, they quickly proliferate through the system, to everyone's benefit, except the Treasury's. Even if the cost per episode goes down, total system spending rises.

The dynamic is illustrated by a new technology, announced in the summer of 1995, that promises to make even heart bypass surgery minimally invasive. A laparoscopy-type procedure—the insertion of a small tube with remote-control instruments and a camera—will eliminate the necessity of breaking the patient's breastbone, opening the chest, and exposing the heart. (Most of the infections, complications, and recovery time from bypasses derive from the terrible collateral damage that the procedure inflicts.) Few specialists appear to doubt that the procedure will work. Bypasses will become cheaper, complications will be reduced, recoveries will be much faster—patients should be out of the hospital in just a couple of days. Inevitably, the procedure will also be resorted to much more frequently than at present.

The radical change in the nature of medical practice has been largely ignored in the political debates over health care. The focus on the apparent runaway growth in health care "costs" is a symptom of the confusion. The Brookings Institution health economist Henry Aaron has pointed out that we can measure only changes in health care *expenditures*, not changes in health care costs. Changing technologies make the mix of services from one time period to the next so radically different that apples-to-apples cost comparisons are impossible.

### *Wishful Thinking*

The more enthusiastic proponents of managed care and HMOs as a magic bullet against cost increases are likely to be seriously disappointed. In a typical HMO, although there are many variations of the principle, a physician pool is paid a flat rate for each patient enrolled that covers the cost of all care. The financial incentive is therefore on the physician to ensure against wasteful duplication of services or unnecessary procedures.

Much of the apparent savings from HMO-style medicine probably relates to the tendency of HMO patients to be healthier. HMOs usually limit the choice of specialist physicians to plan doctors. Patients with an established relationship with a specialist physician, like a cardiologist or an oncologist, are more likely to stick with traditional indemnity-type insurance so they can keep their doctor. But patients with established relationships with cardiologists and oncologists are the ones who are likely to be sickest. One study of Medicare patients who joined HMOs showed that their medical costs were 23 percent lower than the Medicare average the year *before* they joined the HMO.

The first round of government experiments with HMOs for Medicare patients has actually lost money. As a presumed incentive to lower cost, the reimbursement rate for Medicare HMO patients was set at 95 percent of the Medicare average. But since the HMO patients used many fewer services than the average, the HMOs got a windfall. And since some of the lowest-cost patients were removed from the normal system, the average cost of the rest of the population went up. AARP's Rother says he generally supports the Republicans' emphasis on managed care—"It can be *better* care when done right"—but doubts that it will save very much money.

A recent survey in the *Lancet* suggests that, under the pressure of competition, the most successful HMOs are becoming much more like traditional indemnity plans, in allowing free choice of specialist physicians, for example, in order to compete for patients. Quite likely, as HMOs broaden their panels and build their patient populations to the point where they are indistinguishable from those of the indemnity plans, the costs of HMOs and traditional insurance will tend to converge. Some recent data also suggest that HMOs clamp a tighter lid on doctor pay scales. That's one way to generate savings, but it's not quite the same as managing treatment more efficiently.

Another highly touted path to reform is to place more of the initial, or "first-dollar" payment responsibility on the patient. A much-cited Rand study demonstrates that relatively modest deductibles and copayments have a marked effect on lowering patients' recourse to their doctor, by as much as 25 to 30 percent on average. (A "deductible" makes the patient responsible for the first-dollar cost of treatment; a "copayment" means the patient shares the cost of the treatment with the insurer.) A modest deductible of $100 to $200 per year, and a copayment of 20 to 25 percent of the first $1,000, were quite effective inhibitors of system usage, and do not seem onerous. Nor was there any apparent difference in the health of the patients subject to the deductibles and copayments. Over the past several years, America's largest companies, which typically had the most generous health care plans, have almost all imposed much greater employee cost-sharing, which may have contributed to a marked slowdown in business health care costs.

One of the unexciting conclusions of the Rand study, however, was that most private insurance programs already *have* a fairly efficient mix of deductibles and copayments. The implications for Medicare are even more attenuated by the popularity of "Medigap" policies, which pay for most Medicare deductibles and copayments. Once a senior has Medicare and a good Medigap policy she has no incentive to curb utilization. But no one has suggested that the government ban Medigap policies.

In recent years, the most-resorted-to device for constraining Medicare expenditures has been simply to mandate Medicare fee reductions. About three quarters of all Medicare curtailments of the past dozen years have been imposed on providers rather than beneficiaries. That strategy is rapidly approaching its limits, although it is still the key element in the Republican "reform" proposals. The gap between Medicare fee schedules and private schedules has grown apace. In effect, there has been a shift in costs from Medicare to private insurance patients, which is tantamount to a hidden Medicare tax. More and more physicians, moreover, are refusing to take Medicare patients because of the great fee disparities. The longer-term consequence could be a gradual sorting of Medicare patients toward a medical backwater staffed by the least experienced or least competitive doctors.

Any hope that tinkering at the edges of the current health care system can result in significant change in the trend line of future costs is refuted, finally, by examining the distribution of health care costs. In any year, *almost all* health care spending is accounted for by a relatively small percentage of very sick people. A detailed study that broke out all spending for the year 1987, for example, showed that only 1 percent of the population consumed 30 percent of all medical spending, and only 10 percent accounted for fully 72 percent of all spending. Most people had few, if any, encounters with the health care system at all—half the population consumed only 3 percent of total health care spending. A 1992 study of two health insurance companies showed an even greater concentration of claimants—the 1 percent of all patients who had claims greater than $25,000 accounted for half of all claims value.

Other studies suggest that a quarter to a third of all spending occurs in the last year of life, and that within the high-spending groups, older people cost about twice as much as younger people, presumably because they get sicker, tend to have multiple conditions, don't recover as quickly, and are more likely to die. The Rand study, moreover, suggests that while forms of coverage will affect initial utilization of the system, there is no effect on costs or treatment protocols for people who are very sick. Cancer patients receiving care from HMOs are treated pretty much the same as cancer patients with traditional coverage. In short, very sick people account for most of the system's spending, and spending on the very sick is not much affected by the design of insurance programs.

There is no escaping the conclusion that while administrative reforms might temporarily slow the growth of health costs and improve efficiency, and may possibly even improve the quality of care, it is medical technology, not administrative practices, that are driving the continued increase in costs. As Henry Aaron has bluntly put it, "Sustained reductions in the growth of health care spending can be achieved only if some beneficial care is denied to some [presumably deserving] people."

## *Can Care Be Rationed?*

All other industrialized countries have controlled the growth of health care costs by one form or another of rationing. It is not clear how much longer the strategy will work. Costs in Canada, for instance, have been growing faster than in America, although Canadian costs per capita are still lower. Care is rarely rationed directly. In England, for instance, there are stringent limits on local health authority budgets, and officials must decide what kind of care they can provide within the money available. For the most part, the choices have been skewed toward primary care, such as general practitioner coverage, obstetrics, and emergency care. The London ambulance corps, for example, is still superb. But the high-technology interventions that are routine in America are not nearly so available. Rationing is accomplished by queuing. The services that are in official favor have a short waiting period; those that are not have a long one.

The same phenomenon recurs in other countries. Expensive new therapies are simply not funded at all, or funded on a very low level, so they never become routine. Care may fall short of some desirable theoretical ideal, but since patients expect nothing better, they are satisfied, or at least quiescent. The wealthy fly to America for treatment, or pay out-of-pocket for upper-class private care.

The American approach has been totally different. For the entire postwar period, government funds have been lavished on the health care sector—on medical research, facilities construction, specialist training.

Special initiatives, like the national cancer initiative of the 1970s, quite consciously created a chain of government-funded high-technology cancer centers throughout the country, specifically designed to advance the cause of high-technology medicine. Similar initiatives have been pursued in cardiac care, neonatal and perinatal care, and more recently in AIDS and immunological disorders. Patent and licensing arrangements have encouraged the commercialization of government-sponsored research in molecular biology, pharmaceuticals, and diagnostic techniques. The pursuit of profit is readily accepted as the most efficient means of proliferating innovation and new technologies. Doctors, venture capitalists, and investment bankers routinely break bread with each other.

The federal government has recently embarked on an all-court press to unravel the mysteries of Alzheimer's disease, with at least sixteen federal agencies involved in some form of Alzheimer's research. Major drug companies view Alzheimer's as a major target of opportunity, because the potential return from an effective drug will be enormous. Although there is currently little prospect of finding a cure any time soon—the mechanisms of the disease are still very poorly understood—therapies will inevitably become available that will delay the onset of the disease, ease some of the symptoms, and prolong patients' lives. At least one drug that may temporarily slow the progression of the disease and improve memory functions has already been approved by the FDA. Just as inevitably, the national medical bill for Alzheimer's will rise. As Moynihan suggests, the rise in spending is not a sign of failure. The misfortune is merely that our fondest wishes are coming true.

There are clearly rationing targets of opportunity. The most promising, perhaps, is the vast skew of spending toward terminal illness, the seemingly mindless technological imperative to invest all possible resources to prolong any life, however enfeebled or degraded by dysfunction and disease. AARP seminars and instructional materials on trusteeships, living wills, health care proxies, and other devices to allow terminal patients to refuse late-stage technological interventions always draw enthusiastic responses. It appears that many old people facing a final illness would prefer to die more quickly, with more dignity, and less expensively than is now so often the case. There are some signs that the medical ethics regarding end-stage treatment interventions are slowly changing. Disappointingly for reformers, a study recently reported in the *New England Journal of Medicine* suggests that the longer-term savings from reform of terminal illness protocols may not be quite as large as once hoped.

## LONG-TERM CARE

The mainstream congressional debate over the future of Medicare has for the most part simply ignored the looming issue of long-term care. As of this writing, the Republican budget proposals finesse the issue of Medic*aid*, as opposed to Medicare, by converting it into a block grant for the states. The problem is that

Medicaid is the largest single source of funds for nursing homes and other forms of long-term care for the elderly and the disabled. About $108 billion was spent on all forms of long-term care in 1993, including a range of services from nursing homes to home health care; 70 percent of the money paid for institutional care of one form or another. About a third of the cost of long-term care was met by private parties, almost entirely on an out-of-pocket basis. The contribution from private insurance was negligible. The remaining two thirds of the financing came from the government, most from the federal government, and most through Medicaid. Medicaid now pays for about six out of every ten nursing home beds in the country. (In general, Medicare will finance up to sixty days of nursing care; from that point the patient pays out-of-pocket until her assets are "spent down," at which point coverage is picked up by Medicaid.)

The breakup of the traditional extended family, the tendency of older people not to live with, or even near, their adult children, and the wholesale entry of married women into the labor force have all contributed to the growth of nursing homes. A generation or two ago, the addled old grannie living in the family attic was a staple of family folklore. The nursing home industry is merely part of a larger movement toward socializing processes once carried out within families.

The more important dynamic, however, is the sharp increase in the life expectancy of the aged. Eighty-year-olds have been the fastest-growing segment of the population for a couple of decades now. (One of the key actuarial assumptions buried in the Medicare trustees' projection of elderly health care costs is that the increase in life expectancies for the aged has about reached its limits, although there is no way to predict that, one way or the other.) Families could more readily cope with live-in aging relatives in past generations, partly because older people died a lot earlier than they do now.

The sad truth is that even people who are active and healthy in their seventies become frail and dependent in their eighties. Only about 3 percent of people between the ages of sixty-five and seventy-four have Alzheimer's disease, but nearly half of eighty-five-year-olds display symptoms of one form of dementia or another. Paradoxically, the healthiest sixty-five-year-olds are the *most* likely to need nursing home care at some point in their lives, for the simple reason that they are likeliest to live longer. The aging of the boomers will double the number of elderly people in the population, but, because of longer life expectancies, the number of people requiring long-term care is expected to increase by a factor of *five*, from fewer than 5 million at present to nearly 25 million.

The distribution of nursing home costs displays the same pattern as in the rest of the health care industry. Epidemiological projections for the cohort of people who turned sixty-five in 1990 forecast that almost half of the cohort, 43 percent, will need nursing home care at some point in their lives. About half of the people who enter nursing homes will be there less than a year, most for less than three months, either because they recover sufficiently to return to independent living, or they die. But 18 percent of the cohort will spend more than two years in a nursing home—9 percent more than five years—and they will account for 90 percent of the cohort's total nursing home costs. They are also the most seriously disabled, and the least likely candidates for lower-cost alternatives like home health care.

The present value of the cost of nursing home care for the 1990 "class" of sixty-five-year-olds is estimated to be about $60 billion. That is to say, if $60 billion were salted away today at market interest rates, there would be enough money available to pay for all the 1990 class's nursing home needs as they aged. Since the number of people turning sixty-five will be fairly flat for the rest of the decade, a similar amount, in today's dollars, would be enough to fund each new year's class. As the boomers begin to retire, however, *and* nursing home usage rises as new retiring cohorts live longer, the numbers grow sharply, to perhaps a quarter of a trillion dollars each year in *today's* dollars. That is a sobering thought.

The lack of attention being paid to the long-term care problem is the more striking because there is probably no issue of greater salience to the aged. The present generation of healthy seniors, the kind of people who turn out for AARP chapter meetings, are managing their current health care needs better than any previous generation ever has, after making all allowances for gaps in the system. But almost none of them has long-term care insurance, and Alzheimer's and nursing home care lurk in the background, like some huge threatening shadow. At the moment, policymakers on both sides of the congressional aisle are doing their best to avert their eyes.

In a few years, the limits of the current reform initiatives will be too obvious to ignore. Cost growth in Medicare will *necessarily* outstrip health care cost growth as a whole for the simple reason that almost all Medicare patients are old. Sixty-five-year-olds use a lot more medical services than forty-year-olds, and eighty-year-olds need *much* more service even than sixty-five-year-olds. Eighty-year-olds are already one of the fastest-growing American subpopulations, and in about fifteen years, the over-sixty-five population will explode. At that point, if not before, the nation will be forced to deal more directly with the fundamental questions: How much care? For whom? To what purpose? Before looking at practical reforms, however, it is important to place the question of escalating health care expenditures in a broader economic context. How much of a disaster is it?

# Chapter 8

## *The Transformation of the American Economy*

A FUNDAMENTAL ASSUMPTION OF almost all health care reform proposals is that health care spending is "out of control," that we must quickly apply a social tourniquet and staunch the continued growth of the health care sector or the country will become impoverished. It is time to look at that assumption more closely, for I believe it is seriously wrong.

### OF NEUROSURGEONS AND TAIL FINS

There is a wing of American liberal politics, with roots in British Fabianism, that has long had a romantic attachment to city bus services. Public transportation enthusiasts have always been on the losing side in America. At some point in the 1920s and 1930s, Americans made an unambiguous collective decision enshrining the private automobile as the transportation mode of choice. Older cities, like New York and Philadelphia, were forcibly reshaped to accommodate automobiles, and all newer cities, like those in the

West and Southwest, and all suburbs were designed around the automobile.

The economic implications of the decision in favor of automobiles were profound. The heart of America's midwestern heavy-industry belt—iron and steel, coal and rubber, cement and glass—grew up around the automobile, and powered the American industrial dominance of the 1950s and 1960s. The public subsidies poured into the automobile economy were immense. To replicate the national highway system, the crown jewel of Dwight Eisenhower's domestic policy, would cost trillions in today's dollars. For most of the 1950s and 1960s, the American oil industry, by dint of the notorious oil depletion allowance, was effectively exempt from federal taxation in order to keep gasoline prices low. Industrial unionism—the autoworkers, the steel workers, the rubber workers—and its folklore, like Walter Reuther's great strike of Ford's River Rouge plant, were rooted in the automobile industry. And it was automobile-based heavy manufacturing that fueled the steady rise of American industrial workers into the ranks of the comfortable middle classes.

Calculating the share of the American economy dependent on the automobile in the 1950s and 1960s is hopeless, because the spinoffs were so great: Does one count the expansion of the electric power grid that followed the spread of the highway system across the land? Suffice it to say that it was very large—15 percent would seem a conservative assumption. The cultural consequences of an automotive economy, like the independence conferred on teenagers with driving licenses, were at least as profound as the economic.

A few holdouts among left-leaning economists, like John Kenneth Galbraith, viewed the automotive economy as almost total waste, and they had a good case. As highways multiplied, so did traffic jams. Garish tail fins, three-year product cycles, and planned obsolescence were the antithesis of a cost-effective transportation system. The environmental costs of the highway system, suburban sprawl, and gasoline-engine pollution were incalculable. But Galbraith and his coterie were a cranky minority. By conventional economic standards, the 1950s and 1960s were America's golden age.

Conventional economic measures are built around counting things and money. And by all measures American industrial productivity, American real incomes, and the American standard of living rose as they never have before or since. It seems clear in retrospect that there was never any possibility that Americans could have chosen buses and trains over the freedom and independence of the automobile, despite the many theoretical advantages of public transportation systems. And in view of the enormous increase in national wealth that derived from the automobile industry, it is hard to argue that the choice was wrong.

The analogy between automobiles and health care is closer than it may first appear. The city bus service version of health care is epitomized by the government-sponsored, comprehensive, single-payer, highly rationalized, cost-effective British National Health Service, the prototype of them all. Like bus systems, it costs a lot less than America's tail fin–heavy version of health care, perhaps only a third as much. And like a bus system, there are some places it simply doesn't go. Hip replacements, cataract surgery, heart bypasses, and liver transplants are not routine services in England, or in Canada, the way they are here. In terms of their cost-effectiveness (however that can be measured), neurosurgeons and cosmetic surgeons may be the health industry's equivalent of the chrome-laden car, while dialysis centers, the network of cancer institutes, the massive government investments in teasing out the molecular basis of disease are the 1990s version of the national highway system and the oil depletion allowance—jump starts for an industrial transformation. And it is hard to imagine Americans settling for anything less.

The overriding political problem in America today is the rapid growth in health care costs. So the question that is dominating political debate is, How can we prevent health care from consuming a larger and larger share of our national wealth? Framing the question that way, however, limits the scope of the answer. If the *share* of the economy devoted to health care is the problem, the only solution is to cut the growth of health care. But is that the right way to define the problem? Are we asking the right question?

## "BAUMOL'S DISEASE"

It's not hard to understand the alarm at the relentless rise in American health care spending, and at the steadily growing share of the national economy that health care represents. Health care spending accounted for about 5 percent of the national economy in 1950, but had risen to a more than 10 percent slice of a much larger economy by 1980. By 1995, health care's share of the economy was up to about 15 percent, and it will be closing in on the 20 percent mark by the turn of the decade. In short, about $1 out of every $5 spent in the entire country in the year 2000, whether by consumers, business, or government, will be spent, one way or the other, on health care. The *annual* growth in hospital workers has been about the same as *total* employment in the American computer manufacturing industry.

As long as the health care sector continues to grow faster than the rest of the economy, as it has for decades, its share of national spending must inevitably increase, and the American economy will become—in more ways that one, some fear—a huge hospital ward. Health care is already the nation's biggest industry, passing the $1 trillion "sales" mark in 1994, and American health care is quite likely the *world's* biggest industry. It is taken for granted that a constantly expanding health care sector is an ominous trend, one that cannot possibly be sustained. But if one looks more closely, that conclusion is not quite as obvious as it first seems.

"Baumol's disease" is a characteristic of modern economies first identified almost thirty years ago by two Princeton University economists, William Baumol and William Bowen, and subsequently much elaborated by Baumol. (Baumol prefers the term *cost disease*.) Baumol points out that it is very difficult to increase the productivity of any service with a strong handcrafted element. Classroom teachers, string quartet players, masseurs, and artists all work in enterprises where productivity improvements are very hard to come by. Computerized research bases and modern word processors might improve the productivity of book writers, but not enormously. General practitioners have many more tests at their disposal and can get lab results back much faster, but the time it takes to examine a patient hasn't changed much. Not all services have this characteristic. There are many fewer telephone operators now than fifty years ago, but the system handles vastly more calls. Private companies have also greatly increased the productivity of package delivery. But wherever the handcrafted element dominates, as in chiropractic or kindergarten teaching, productivity will grow very slowly, if at all.

That much, perhaps, is obvious. What is less obvious is that enterprises in which productivity grows slowly tend inevitably to increase their share of the overall economy. Consider an economy that produces only cars and massages. Assume that the productivity of car workers goes up 5 percent a year, and that their wages grow at the same rate. Over time, they will produce many more cars than before, but the price of the cars will not change as long as the wage increases track the productivity increases. Suppose, however, as is likely, that the wages of masseurs rise to keep pace with the wages of autoworkers. Then, the prices of massages will have to rise, because the masseurs won't be producing any more massages than before.

But if the number of autos and massages produced stays roughly the same, and the price of massages rises, and the price of cars doesn't, the dollar-value of massage output will obviously grow much faster than that of car output. When the government statisticians tot up the national economic data at the end of the year, they will show the massage industry steadily increasing its share of national output, and the car industry steadily losing share. Productivity data will be falling, because the low-productivity massage industry will have a bigger share of national product than the high-productivity car makers. Worried economists will write articles about "deindustrialization." But in the real world of goods and services actually produced, nothing much will have changed.

"Baumol's disease" is the inevitable tendency of low-productivity personal services to expand their share of the national economy. Prices in industries that can be readily automated, like the making of television sets, will fall much faster than prices in industries that do not lend themselves to automation, like the production of television shows. As a consequence, low-productivity activity will account for a greater and greater share of total costs. The computer industry is a good recent example. The productivity of computer manufacturing has been rising at an extraordinary rate, at about 25 percent a year, for almost thirty years. But writing computer *software* is still a handcrafted, low-productivity business. Thirty years ago, software costs were such a trivial component of a typical computer installation that computer manufacturers usually gave the software away for free. By the mid-1980s, however, the cost of software in the typical industrial computer installation had grown to the point where it exceeded the cost of the hardware. It is not inconceivable that, in some foreseeable future, computer companies will give away their very cheap hardware in order to sell their much more expensive software. Fast-food chains keep their costs down by limiting the personal-service element. Identical frozen french fries are cooked exactly the same way in every McDonald's outlet; there are no local chefs creating signature dishes; there is no table service.

In any modern economy, therefore, the price of personal services that cannot be easily automated will rise faster than other activities, and will therefore inevitably increase their share of the *nominal* economy—that is, as measured by current prices. "Baumol's disease" is the engine that is driving the rapid expansion of the service sector in every industrialized country, not just in the United States. In America, the service sector has grown to about 70 percent of national product. The process is not quite so advanced elsewhere, but it is not far behind, and in most industrialized countries, including Japan, the rate of growth in the service sector is even faster than in the United States. The steady expansion of the health care sector is only the most dramatic example of "Baumol's disease." Education shows almost exactly the same pattern on a somewhat smaller scale.

As Baumol's thesis would suggest, however, the expansion of the services share is not nearly so dramatic when measured in constant prices. In America, in addition, the "deindustrialization" theorists to the contrary notwithstanding, the share of the total economy accounted for by the real output of manufacturing and other goods-producing industries—that is, correcting for the different rates of price inflation in manufacturing and personal services—has been roughly constant since World War II. Industrial output relative to services has actually been *rising* in the recent past. It is only when measured in inflated dollars, so the "money illusion" effect kicks in, that we see a vast expansion of the service sector. Finally, since manufacturing is a high-productivity undertaking, trends in *employment* make the shift from a goods-producing to a service economy seem even sharper. Although manufacturing's share of constant-dollar output has been quite stable, the percentage of the workforce employed in manufacturing has fallen from 27 percent in 1950 to only 14 percent now, and the total number of manufacturing workers has grown hardly at all, from 16 million workers in 1950 to 18 million now.

Baumol himself first used the word *disease* to describe the inevitability of an expanding service sector. Baumol's own writings suggest that he may regret the choice of words, for he has been among the leaders in questioning whether the phenomenon is really a "disease" at all, or merely a natural attribute of a wealthy economy.

## HEALTH CARE IN A SERVICE-INTENSIVE ECONOMY

To treat the expansion of the health care industry purely as an example of the Baumol thesis oversimplifies the problem. To be sure, giving a patient an alcohol back rub takes the same amount of time as it did fifty years ago, and the nurse, or the nurse's aide, or the physical therapist who gives it gets paid a lot more, in real terms, than he or she once did. (Anecdotal evidence suggests that, in the same way that McDonald's eliminated table service, hospitals have also been limiting low-productivity personal services. Try to find a nurse to give you a back rub in a modern high-tech hospital.)

***Service Productivity*** Almost all economists agree that productivity improvement is the basic source of improvement in economic well-being. If overall labor productivity improves by 5 percent, each worker, at least potentially, can improve her consumption of goods and services by 5 percent, which is what getting richer is all about. (Who actually gets the extra 5 percent, of course, is another story.) But *measuring* productivity turns out to be devilishly difficult. Suppose a worker in a computer factory could produce one personal computer a day that sold for $3,000. And suppose that a couple of years later, he could produce three much more powerful computers that sold for $1,000 each. This is pretty much of a real-world example. Did his productivity go up dramatically, or stay the same? The price-value of his output is still $3,000 a day, but the "quality-value" has gone up by more than three times. Every few years, the Commerce Department, which counts such things, bravely tries to estimate computer quality improvements so it can factor that into the industry's productivity measures.

Quality improvements are much harder to track in a service industry like health care. (In computers, at least, there are standard measures of processing power that can be used as a rough quality index.) In fact, there are ample grounds for believing that health care productivity has been rising, perhaps even rising strongly, but it's hard to prove and even harder to measure.

Hospital stays, for instance, are much shorter than they used to be. Some of the very short stays that have become typical in America, like the day and a half or so that is standard for a normal childbirth, may be overdoing it. But the long hospital stays that are characteristic of many other countries suggest that a lot of bed space is being consumed either in waiting for treatment or in resting up afterward. The short lengths of stay that have become the norm in America also suggest that the average patient is much sicker than elsewhere. People recovering from the acute stage of their illness are sent home, so the bed can be filled with someone in need of intensive treatment. A great many surgical and invasive diagnostic procedures that once necessitated a couple of days in the hospital are now performed on an outpatient basis, which would also increase the average seriousness of in-hospital cases. Finally, the level of technology applied to each patient has also risen sharply. In an economist's terms, the capital investment per patient is very high, and growing rapidly, which is usually associated with rising productivity.

Henry Aaron, for some years now, has been drumming home that we know very little about the extent of health care *cost* increases. We know only that health care *expenditures* have been going up very rapidly, which is not the same thing at all. For example, arthroscopic surgery is now a common procedure for removing calcified debris from major joints. (It is almost routine for professional athletes.) The surgery is invasive, but barely so, involving only a tiny incision and the insertion of a pinhead-sized fiber-optic camera, a microscopic scraping tool, and a miniature suction tube. Twenty years ago, cleaning out a debris-obstructed knee or elbow was a major surgical procedure—the entire joint was opened up and exposed—with attendant risk of infections and other complications, and a comparatively low rate of success. It posed the kind of risk that only a professional athlete could justify taking, and then only when there were no other alternatives. By any reasonable standard, then, the productivity of joint-cleaning therapies has improved dramatically, and the cost per procedure has dropped sharply. *Expenditures* have probably also increased substantially, however (there are no good data on such things), because the new procedure will be resorted to much more frequently, and in much milder cases, than the previous one. Almost the same point could be made about almost any part of the health care system.

Observational data would suggest that the content of what hospital workers do has been changing very fast, just as in other technology-driven industries, like computers or telecommunications. Neurosurgeons in advanced medical centers now simulate upcoming surgical procedures on advanced computer workstations, using MRI mappings of the patient's brain to devise the least damaging route to an object to be excised. Laser scalpels can burn away a pinhead-sized brain tumor with only minimal collateral damage. Until relatively recently, it would not have been possible even to diagnose such a tumor, much less operate on it. If the Commerce Department could track the cost and efficacy of a constant unit of brain surgery, the data would almost certainly show very rapid productivity improvements, but there is no such constant unit.

The same point applies to a very large number of modern procedures, from cataract surgery to hip replacements. Pharmaceuticals that shrink benign swelling of the prostate gland promise to be more cost-effective, with fewer side effects, than old-fashioned surgery. Or consider the cost of the old tuberculosis sanitariums compared to modern antibacillus therapies. Medications against depression and other common psychiatric illnesses have worked revolutions. And in almost every case, as the cost and risk of intervention drops, the universe of potential customers expands apace.

From 1970 to 1986, the number of hospital employees per patient rose by about 45 percent, and their pay rose faster than for other workers. But there is no way to draw definitive conclusions about their productivity, since the change in how they spend their time is too dramatic for comparisons to be meaningful. There is no unit of output, like a car, or a bushel of wheat, that can be used as a convenient index. In service industries that lack a standard unit of output, like education or most government services, the Commerce Department falls back on measuring *inputs*; instead of measuring productivity, it merely measures costs and prices. The lagging productivity of the service sector, therefore, may be substantially overstated, as it almost certainly is in health care. In some categories of health care, like nursing homes or patient examinations, productivity may not have risen very much at all. In others, like standard surgical procedures or the substitution of drugs for expensive surgical or psychotherapeutic interventions, productivity has probably risen very sharply.

"Baumol's disease," therefore, is only part of the story. There are *two* separate engines driving the growth of the health care sector. Any labor-intensive industry that cannot be easily automated will inevitably increase its share of the economy, as Baumol has suggested. But in addition, American health care is technology-driven and technology-intensive and offers a range of rapidly proliferating products and services that, for the most part, enhance people's lives, and which consumers very much want.

## A HEALTH CARE–BASED ECONOMY

A prominent strain of recent American economic commentary implies that the long-term trend to a more services-intensive economy is somehow making America poorer. In perhaps slightly exaggerated form, it runs like this: Services are pure consumption that draw capital away from our industrial base, and the accelerating trend toward a personal services economy undermines productivity, which is the fundamental source of all wealth and economic advancement. The apparently inexorable advance of a future where 20 percent, or even a third, of our national economic activity is devoted to health care looks like an unmitigated disaster, trapping a large portion of our workforce in dead-end, low-wage service jobs—portending a nation of nurses' aides and hamburger flippers. We therefore need to bring health care spending "under control" before it saps our industrial productivity any further, and devote our scarce capital to creating *real* jobs, especially *manufacturing* jobs. It is a view that spans the political spectrum. The "industrial policy" wing of the Democratic Party worries about our international competitiveness, while conservatives worry that health care's claim on federal revenues will bury the economy under an avalanche of debt.

There is a grain of truth in the argument. The more people who are working in what Baumol calls the "stagnant services," where productivity improvement is almost impossible, like kindergarten teachers or masseurs, the slower overall productivity can grow and the less net new wealth can be produced. But for the most part, the argument that a continued shift away from traditional heavy industry toward health care will somehow impoverish the country is a compound of nonsense. It is worth examining in some detail.

***The Jobs Argument*** There is a prevailing perception that service jobs are poorly paying, dead-end jobs. As a general proposition, it is simply not true. Service jobs, on average, pay less than manufacturing jobs but more than jobs in retail trade. The manufacturing averages are skewed by the shrinking base of elite, unionized, CIO-style jobs (in the late 1970s, cafeteria workers at Bethlehem Steel, who were represented by the Steelworkers' Union, got paid $20 an hour). But "service" jobs also cover a very wide range, from stockbrokers and telecommunications workers down to the minimum-wage busboy or the proverbial hamburger flipper. In general, workers in industries with large amounts of invested capital per worker, whether in manufacturing or services, get paid more than workers in low-investment industries. The additional capital not only helps them produce more, but employers have too much capital at risk to entrust it to low-skill, low-wage people.

Health care is rapidly becoming a capital-intensive industry. Hospitals account for about 35 percent of all health care expenditure, and are the biggest single component of national health care spending. The cost of a hospital stay, however, has been rising much faster than the pay of hospital workers. The extra money is being applied *both* to increase the capital investment per patient *and* the number of workers per patient. The phenomena are related: The proliferation of diagnostic equipment requires an increase in diagnostic equipment technicians. As a consequence, the job profile of the average hospital worker is beginning to look more like that of a telecommunications worker—handling expensive and specialized equipment that requires expensive on-the-job or certificated training—than that of a hamburger flipper or custodian. As one would expect, health care workers, on average, get paid somewhat more than the average American worker, and hospital workers get about 30 percent more than the average.

From an employment perspective, health care has the additional advantage of being mostly nontradable. The high earnings of American manufacturing workers inevitably mean that America's natural competitive advantage will be in capital-intensive production—semiconductors, specialized chemicals, petrochemical equipment, high-end capital goods—

that is steadily reducing its raw labor content. At the same time, low-capital-intensive production, like the needle trades and light consumer product assembly, will gravitate to lower-wage countries. In a mature economy operating in an open trading system, therefore, employment in industries producing tradable goods will tend to shrink. American manufacturing productivity, in fact, has been quite high for more than a decade, but the inevitable consequence has been a shrinking manufacturing workforce.

Health care, in happy contrast, offers not only better-than-average pay, but rapidly growing employment opportunities, including a wide range of skilled and semiskilled technician jobs that require training and intelligence but usually not advanced degrees. Economists have long lamented the loss of the skilled and semiskilled manufacturing jobs that underpinned the prosperity of America's working-class families for so many years. Where will the new jobs come from to fuel the rise of the newer generations of immigrant and minority workers? It is hard to think of any sector of the economy that offers opportunities comparable to those in health care. There are now more than 10 million workers employed in the health care industry, or about 50 percent more than the number employed in automobile and automobile-related industries.

Health care has the additional advantage of offering a somewhat more egalitarian earnings pattern than many other industries. Doctors and hospital administrators earn good salaries, but the spread between the top and bottom earners in health care is nowhere near as great as at General Motors. Competitive pressures within the industry, from the proliferation of HMOs and similar structural changes, have kept doctors' earnings roughly flat in real terms for more than a decade.

There is still the nagging question: Can we *afford* the growth in health care employment? How can the increased consumption of health care produce "real wealth" the way manufacturing workers do?

***Counting Conventions and Other Biases*** It is much easier to measure things than services. In the decades when America's central economic activity was converting to an automobile-based economy, one could easily count the new cars rolling down the assembly lines, the tons of ore being converted into steel, the barrels of petroleum refined into gasoline, the miles of new highways, the new houses in tract developments. Much of this, as Galbraith insisted, was waste—ugly cars that were too big, used too much gas, spewed out too much pollution, destroyed too much landscape. But economists unhesitatingly counted it all as new *wealth.* When an older person gets a hip replacement or cataract surgery, however, it does not appear so obviously on the radar screen as an increase in wealth. The counting conventions simply log more spending going into the low-productivity service sector—pure consumption. The stock of goods does not increase. The new hip or the cleared vision does not go onto the national balance sheet as a household asset the way a car or a house does—even though they may enhance life and confer personal freedom as much as a new car ever did.

There is a brawny illusion about manufacturing and other goods-producing industries that makes them seem more "real" than services. To take an example, industrial production was flat through much of the spring of 1995, but rose in the summer, an upturn that was widely hailed as presaging a recovery. Actually, the new industrial output was entirely accounted for by extra power production due to air-conditioning usage during the hot summer months. It is worth dwelling on what that entailed. Coal was gouged out of western mountainsides, crushed and loaded onto miles-long freight trains, or mixed with millions of gallons of water to flow through slurry pipelines. Oil wells in the North Sea, Alaska, and the Middle East pumped crude oil into giant tankers and pipelines, and transshipped it to refineries throughout the world. Giant coal- and oil-powered turbines fed megawatts of power into the national grid from whence it flowed into millions of air-conditioner motors. And the net result of all this violent activity was that cool air was briefly wafted over Americans' sweaty brows before being vented away to dissipate in the outdoor smog.

But since units of energy production can be precisely measured, total factor inputs of capital and labor carefully logged, rising productivity enthusiastically charted, the cold air blowing through, say, a law firm's offices is taken to represent net new wealth in a way that back rubs for bedridden nursing home patients never can. An alarmed Commerce Department report recently stated: "If the United States were able through health care reform to achieve a level of spending comparable to other countries, the United States could save about 4% of GDP. Those savings could be reallocated to investments in other areas, such as training and production." It is almost certain that the

Commerce Department has never speculated on the GDP that could be "saved" by reducing car production.

What kind of "production" could we afford if we could "save" another 4 percent of GDP? The biggest news on the company front over the past year was the $19 billion Disney–Capital Cities/ABC merger, and the subsequent hiring of Michael Ovitz as president for a $30 million salary package. Hard on the heels of this came news of another blockbuster merger, between Time Warner and Turner Broadcasting. Some of the hottest products in the private economy are $120 air-pump sneakers, "Doom II" video games, and interactive porn. One of the nation's biggest technological challenges—one that is attracting tens of billions in new investment each year—is how to pump thousands of movies into the homes of couch potatoes. Leaving aside distributional issues related to the very poor, the great majority of Americans have pretty much all the housing, cars, television sets, and convenience foods they can use, so an increasing portion of surplus income is being spent on entertainment and high-tech consumer goods, the playthings of an advanced economy. But it is "production," nonetheless, and quite sophisticated, advanced production at that. When one considers the advanced computer and communications technology and the enormous salaries and bonuses that support computer-based index arbitrage and other cutting-edge financial technologies, health care doesn't look so wasteful or so unaffordable.

Moreover, the portion of the health care industry

that does represent measurable, tradable goods is an area in which the United States excels. Taken together, the manufacture and shipment of pharmaceuticals, diagnostic substances, and medical supplies and equipment, at an annual production rate of about $100 billion, is about two thirds as big as the automotive industry, and growing much faster than traditional manufacturing. Health care–related manufacturing has one of the highest technology contents of any industry, and a very high rate of productivity growth.

In contrast to the automotive and consumer electronics industries, American medical equipment and pharmaceuticals are consistent net export earners, with about a $4 billion trade surplus in 1993. There is also a substantial "invisible export" of health care services in terms of the foreign exchange earned when wealthy foreigners come to America for treatment. America spends about $30 billion a year in health care research and development, an amount that compares favorably with any other industry. All trends in other industrialized countries suggest a rapid expansion of the health care sector, much as in America, although with a substantial lag. America, that is, has a leadership position in one of the world's most rapidly growing industries.

A few other concerns may be briefly mentioned. Does the cost of health care in America disadvantage American exports? American exports, in fact, have been rising strongly for more than a decade and American labor costs per unit of output are among the lowest of our developed-country trading partners—lower than in either Japan or Germany, for instance. Health care costs may be a source of disadvantage in certain specific industries, like car manufacturing, for instance, because of long-standing, very rich health care plans that encourage wasteful system usage. The solution, of course, is for the automobile companies to fix their health care plans, not to try to reduce national health care spending.

Is health care absorbing capital that should be devoted to manufacturing and other goods-producing industries? In the first place, it is not obvious why producing more cool air from air conditioners, or more cars with tape decks and four-wheel drives, is inherently preferable to producing more pharmaceutical research and hip replacements. Similarly, there is no reason to believe that the billions of private capital flowing into for-profit hospital chains and HMOs is somehow being used less efficiently than the private capital flowing into hotel chains, record companies, the manufacture of CD-ROM players, or the creation of Internet chat groups. More important, there is no evidence of a capital shortage in the United States. Gross nonresidential fixed investment as a share of GDP, for example, is now higher than it was in the 1950s and 1960s, and the cost of capital—interest rates and the dividends and earnings-dilution cost of issuing new stock—is as low as it has been for decades.

The notoriously low American household savings rate is frequently cited as evidence of low American capital formation. But the savings rate calculation excludes some very large items, like unrealized capital gains in real estate or the financial markets, and contributions to state and local pension funds. The hundreds of billions of new money flowing into mutual funds and the stock market are surely coming from somewhere. (It's not coming from overseas; Japan, for example, has been withdrawing capital from America for several years to shore up its shaky financial sector at home.) In short, there is little or no evidence that increased investment in health care has been to the detriment of the rest of the economy.

## CAN THE HEALTH CARE SECTOR KEEP GROWING?

The simple answer is "yes." American health care is an advanced, capital-intensive, well-paying, rapidly expanding sector of the economy, perhaps the largest single source of new middle-class jobs without elitist entry requirements. It may be entirely appropriate, in fact, to turn the question around. Can we afford *not* to sustain and encourage a continued healthy growth of the health care industry?

Certainly, it is hard to think of any advantage to be gained from *curtailing* health care's growth. It will be important to end waste and fraud, and eliminate inappropriate treatments and price gouging. But the simplistic proposition that health care is inherently a drain on the rest of the economy doesn't withstand analysis. If we somehow discovered the magic bullet that would put a stop to the continued expansion of the health care sector, it is hard to imagine why we would want to use it, or of any reason why we would thereby be better off. But it is possible to think of a great many reasons why we would be poorer.

But accepting the proposition that the continued rapid growth of health care is a *good* thing, not a bad thing, still leaves a host of difficult problems relating to the structuring and the financing of the industry, which we will turn to in the next chapter.

# Chapter 9

## *Paths to Reform*

### A WALK ON THE SUNNY SIDE

DISCUSSIONS ABOUT THE FUTURE of senior entitlements tend to veer between extremes of apocalypticism and complacency. For an example of the complacent approach, consider a recent article by Theodore Marmor and Jerry Mashaw, two Yale professors, who are among the most intelligent liberal analysts of entitlement programs:

> What Medicare covers should be broadened to include the burdensome costs of chronic illness; that means incorporating prescription drugs and long-term care into the program.... Widening the benefit package does not mean that total expenditures must rise proportionately.... Other nations have universal insurance with broader benefits, but spend less per elderly citizen than we do. They are able to do this because they pay their medical professionals less, spend less on administration, and use expensive

> technology less often. . . . There is no good reason why [Medicare's] outlays need to rise at twice the rate of general inflation—or more.

As should be clear from chapter 7, the professors have cavalierly dismissed all the hard problems with a few throwaway phrases like "use expensive technology less often." Making all due allowances for the waste in the system, the spending growth is driven by health care that *works*. It is only theoretically true that other countries have broader senior medical benefits than America does—in most enlightened industrial democracies, older people either wait at the end of the line for their hip replacements, dialysis treatment, or organ transplants, or don't get them at all. If we are going to "use expensive technology less often," there must be some principles, and some mechanism, for deciding who will not be treated with that expensive technology, and *that* is the hard problem that no one has yet figured out how to solve.

For some decades, all of our health care policies have been devoted wholeheartedly to the task of bringing expensive technology to bear on more and more people. The American government has devoted hundreds of billions in public subsidies, and American industry has invested hundreds of billions more, in improving health care technology and making it more widely available. The net result is a very expensive but, procedure for procedure, a very effective system of care. In America, the consumers' test is the ultimate one, and there are few old people who think they shouldn't get the same access to high-technology, capital-intensive care as everyone else. They have seen their friends with angioplasties, hip replacements, and cataract surgery, they know those treatments work, and they want them for themselves.

As Brookings's Henry Aaron has consistently argued, the only way to cut the growth of spending in a substantial, permanent way is to begin to deny useful services to worthy people. That is not an easy problem, morally or mechanically. (Should we fund the new prescription drug benefits that Marmor and Mashaw want by eliminating prosthetic implants, or bypasses, or dialysis, for people over seventy, or over seventy-five? Should we, in principle, not employ artificial life support for eighty-year-olds? Should liver and heart transplants be limited to people under fifty?) The elaborate cost containment mechanisms of the Clinton health care reform bill represented one pass at the problem, but it was deemed, probably correctly, to be of indigestible complexity—a way to avoid facing difficult decisions by burying them in bureaucracy. There are no simple, brilliant solutions that could be readily implemented if only the Congress weren't so dumb.

It is unfair, of course, to single out Marmor and Mashaw. Conservative Republicans have their own version of the complacency school. In counterpoint to the Marmor/Mashaw column quoted, conservative commentator Cal Thomas argued that all problems would go away if Medicare were turned over to private insurance companies, which is ridiculous. Both conservatives and liberals will come closer to the path of honesty if they admit that it is health care successes, not government failures, that are powering spending.

## DÉJÀ VU ALL OVER AGAIN

The opposite of excessive complacency is apocalypticism. A staff report from the Concord Coalition, a citizens' group organized by investment banker Peter Peterson, for example, has made a series of careful projections showing that, on quite reasonable economic assumptions, taxes to support Social Security and Medicare could consume a full 85 percent of payrolls by the year 2030, the peak period of boomer dependence on the system. On its own terms, the staff report is an excellent piece of economic analysis, and its value is to point up some of the very optimistic assumptions built into the Social Security and Medicare trustees' demographic and cost growth projections. No one could take it seriously as a projection, however—the authors themselves don't. The country is not going to reach the point where 85 percent, or even 50 to 60 percent of payrolls are devoted to Social Security and Medicare, for the simple reason that working people have to eat and buy shoes, too.

Apocalyptic projections tend to ignore built-in systemic limits. One can easily show that: (a) when the boomers retire, if seniors have the same access to care as they do now, and (b) if technology continues to expand the range of potentially effective treatments at the same rate as in the recent past, *then* the cost of the health care will consume some impossibly large fraction of the economy *unless* we make radical changes in the system of health care provision.

But the prosaic truth is that, while spending on health care will undoubtedly continue to grow, it will not reach an impossibly large fraction of the economy *whether or not we do anything.*

The impact of the boomers on the educational system offers a direct historical analogy to their coming impact on health care. It is safe to say that no one ever loved the boomers more than their parents did, nor has anyone so loved them since. In the child-centered decades of the 1950s and 1960s, boomer parents had no higher priority than the education of their children. But in terms of physical provision, boomers got a decidedly second-rate product.

Despite the abiding concern of their parents for the boomers' welfare, despite their willingness to sustain heroic increases in property taxes, the system simply could not respond fast or flexibly enough. The boomers were forced to endure grossly overcrowded classrooms, double and triple school sessions, long bus rides to regional schools, and a host of other daily indignities. Spending on education rose very sharply in the 1950s and 1960s, of course, but it did not rise nearly fast enough to provide the individualized, activity-rich, educational programming that boomer parents hoped for. (As the system belatedly began to catch up, late-stage boomers, and certainly the much smaller generation of children who followed them, were subjected to more curriculum enrichments, counseling, and psychologic attentions than anyone could be expected to survive unscathed.)

The same phenomenon will recur when aging boomers hit the health care system. Twenty-five million nursing home beds will not appear overnight. Teacher shortages were patched over in the 1950s by occasionally pressing bright high school graduates into service, but it takes a long time to produce a neurosurgeon. Double sessions in classrooms are a lot easier than in operating rooms. Class sizes are almost infinitely expandable—1950s city parochial schools often had a hundred children to a class—but nursing homes can't stack their patients two to a bed. As with schools, stubborn institutional and systemic obstacles will create long lags between the time a service need becomes urgent and the new panoply of services actually rolls into place. The result will be a rough-and-ready, probably fairly random, form of care rationing by queuing. The systemic limits to expanding the health care provision is just one more example of Herbert Stein's dictum that "unsustainable trends tend not to be sustained." The consequence will be less than optimum care for boomers, far less so than for the present generation of seniors. But who said the world was supposed to be just?

## THE SENIOR ENTITLEMENTS PROBLEM IS VERY SERIOUS; IT IS NOT A CRISIS

What follows is a plea for treating seniors' entitlement programs with all the gravity they deserve as the country's most important public policy challenge, while at the same time muffling some of the more alarmist statements of the problem. The trust funds have been going "bankrupt" for decades. No one really believes it, and they're right not to. Republican clamor about a "crisis" in Medicare sits poorly next to their proposals for large tax cuts—roughly equaling the Medicare cuts—and more spending on military hardware that the Pentagon doesn't want. To begin with, we should be clear on what is and is not a problem.

*A Nonproblem* The increase in health care spending *by itself* is not a problem. Capital-intensive, high-technology medicine is one of the strongest growth areas of the economy, the best single source of decent-paying, private-sector jobs, a ready path up into middle-class status for new generations of minorities, immigrants, and other lower-income people. Health care spending is not a *drain* on the economy, no more than flashy cars and eight-lane highways were. It will be no disaster if health care spending eventually consumes as much as a third of national output. Distributional issues aside, only a very small percentage of output is truly required to support basic human needs. We *should* be concerned about true health care waste and inappropriate treatment, like keeping a dying person on expensive life support systems beyond all dictates of decency and common sense. But we should not set out to reduce health care costs for its own sake, on the misbegotten theory that health care somehow weakens the economy in a way that, say, video games or new Windows 95 software don't.

At some point, the reallocation of national resources toward health care would cut into other forms of "surplus" consumption, but there is no obvious reason why that should be a bad thing. If older people have to buy slightly smaller recreational vehicles, or younger people buy fewer (imported) designer jeans and $100+ sneakers to fund the shift of resources, so be it. Health care is one of the few industries that is both an intensive user of technology *and* requires lots of skilled and semiskilled workers. Baumol guesses that the expansion of the health sector's share of the economy will begin to bump into impassable bottlenecks at about the 30 to 35 percent mark. He admits it's a guess, but it seems plausible enough. At that point, no matter how many people are convinced that they *need* a new knee or a nursing home bed, the system will no longer be able to produce them at a sufficient rate. Even if we wanted to spend more, we won't.

***Some Nonsolutions*** There is a strain of wishful thinking in American politics with a penchant for "comprehensive" solutions to big problems. But the number of times the country has actually implemented comprehensive solutions to problems of the scale of health care can be counted on the fingers of one hand: the creation of the Social Security system, the Marshall Plan, the national highway system. The notion that a few smart people—or a lot of smart people—can go into a room, or have a debate in Congress, and reform the American health care "system" is a seductive one, but it is the path to folly. This is a trillion-dollar industry, with more than 10 million employees. Compared to other industries, like food or cars, we have remarkably little hard information on it. It is extremely decentralized, and detailed data on what doctors and hospitals actually *do*, and how they decide to do it, is quite sparse.

And even if we had *lots* of data, the idea that a small group of intellectuals could come up with a few simple ways to make the entire system work better and more cheaply is unrealistic to say the least. There are, of course, many improvements that can be made. The point is simply that they will have to be made piecemeal. The 1990 congressional mandate standardizing Medigap insurance offerings is a good example of a successful, important, piecemeal reform. Medicare's flat-rate diagnosis-based system of reimbursing hospitals, despite a rocky start, seems to be another. By itself, it was quite complex, but it had a substantial impact on hospital practices, and seems to have exerted a real, if temporary, downward pressure on costs. When we resist piecemeal reform, we make the theoretical best the enemy of an achievable good. Muddling through may be inelegant, but it is the true art of government. At least temporarily, the idea of "comprehensive" health care reform seems to be off the political table. The wiser course may be to leave it there.

The same observations apply to the broader issue of "entitlement reform." The 1994 Bipartisan Commission on Entitlement and Tax Reform, chaired by Senators Bob Kerrey and John Danforth, despite producing much useful research, could not muster sufficient internal agreement even to produce a majority report. The even broader recommendations of the Concord Coalition, which have the great virtue of turning the spotlight on *all* entitlements, including those dispensed to the wealthier members of society, seem likewise doomed to the dustbin by their very comprehensiveness.

As of early 1996, therefore, it seems the course of wisdom to recognize that there is no possibility of a comprehensive reform of entitlement programs in the near term. Particularly in the health care arena, the reforms required are of such a scale as to require large bipartisan majorities to be effective, even if we knew what to do. Election-year politics alone make the formation of any such broad consensus impossible for the foreseeable future. The policy challenge is not to develop brilliant, sweeping schemes, but to commit to the long, gritty, sweaty work of gradually putting into place, over a number of years, a series of consistent, piecemeal reforms.

***The Permissible Limits of Reform*** Reformers who ignore the changed context of politics in America will do so at their peril, and probably doom their efforts to failure. We live in the age of the pollster, and there is quite a lot of information about what Americans think about Social Security and Medicare, and much is also known about the attitudes of Americans toward the government and the medical profession.

There are no other government programs that enjoy the same level of support that Social Security and Medicare do. No others even come close. Recent *New York Times*/CBS polls, for instance, showed that strong majorities favor reducing budget deficits and cutting taxes, but *not* if it requires cutting Medicare or Social Security. The margins in favor of protecting Medicare were four to one, an extraordinary level of support; those in favor of protecting Social Security were three to one, still extremely high.

Support for Medicare and Social Security cuts across all groups. Indeed, it is *stronger* among younger people than among seniors. AARP has commissioned dozens of polls on this issue. "Support for the program is always higher among people under sixty-five than over sixty-five. Always. Always been that way," says Rother. Younger people worry about their ability to support aging parents, they worry about their ability to save enough for their own retirements, and they want the programs to be there for themselves "just in case." Significantly, Medicare is viewed as a critical element of *financial* security, even more important than Social Security. There is also a surprisingly high level of support for the payroll tax, rather than the income tax, as a financing mechanism. It's viewed as "fairer" than the income tax system because "there are no loopholes."

A growing, but still-cautious, minority of people, perhaps a third, accept the possibility that the programs may have to be cut in order to save them. Upper-income people are more willing to entertain program cuts than lower-income people, though only by a small margin. But the majority of upper-income people do not think their benefits should be cut—recall the Catastrophic Care fiasco. Madelyn Hochstein, the president of the Daniel Yankelovich Group, who conducts most of AARP's polling, says, "The government and the AARPs of the world have been spreading a myth for fifty or sixty years that these are *earned* benefits, and now those myths are coming home to haunt them. Reeducating people at this point is nearly impossible."

Mistrust of government is pervasive. AARP's Martin Corry recalls that at a recent focus group discussion, the group was asked what the objectives of AARP's lobbying program should be. "Just get them to listen to us," said a woman summing up for the entire group. The public is no longer willing to delegate big issues to politicians, or to its putative lobbyists. Hochstein's polls show the same phenomenon. "It's a new world. People seem to want a kind of participatory democracy. I don't think it's feasible, but there is a huge gap between the leadership and the people."

Only rattlesnakes rank lower than the Congress in public esteem, but doctors don't rank much higher. Republican focus groups disclose "emotional venom" toward the medical profession. Remarkably, Republican polls and the Yankelovich studies for AARP find older people citing precisely the same examples—the "$10 aspirin" and the "$100 bedpan," suggesting that these may be standard hospital practice. As the Republican report puts it: "Everyone has a story to tell. . . . 'I went in for eye surgery and they charged me for an autopsy. I complained and they said, "I'm sorry, Mrs. Colby, but that should have been for an EKG." I told them I didn't have one of those either.' " Hochstein says that seniors uniformly see doctors as excessively greedy, looking for money at every turn. "The doctor used to be God, but not anymore."

More than any other issue, senior entitlement reform gets close to the bone of the relation between the people and the government. Aside from fighting wars, looking after the elderly may be the only thing citizens overwhelmingly agree is a proper federal governmental function. It is no time for grand schemes or fast shuffles.

## PATHS TO REFORM

What follows is a set of nongrandiose, piecemeal, pecking-away-at-the-problem reform proposals that, if implemented steadily over the next three to five years, could move the senior entitlement system along a path that would allow it to both weather the impact of the boomers and maintain the all-important generational compact—workers who fund the retirement of one generation must be able to count on equivalent benefits when they grow old themselves. The list is offered without any pretense that it is perfect, final, or complete in any way, or that it should not be subject to much tugging and hauling. Very few, if any, of the proposals are actually new. But taken together, they suggest the magnitude of the opportunity offered by a muddling-through strategy of reform.

***Social Security*** After the 1996 elections, the White House and the Congress should convene another "Greenspan Commission" to review the finances of the Social Security system. Their brief should *not* be to recommend "comprehensive entitlement reform," and they should *not* attempt to link Social Security and Medicare reform in a single package. The Kerrey Commission has amply demonstrated the impracticality of such sweeping approaches, desirable as they may be in principle. The commission should make recommendations on, among other things:

• *Reasonable expectations for income support for seniors.* For example, pension reforms in the 1970s and 1980s will provide much greater pension income to boomers than to the present generation of retirees. AARP research suggests that, on moderate-growth economic assumptions, retired boomers will have *70 percent more real income in the year 2030* than today's retirees, because they will be much more likely to be receiving income from pensions, Social Security, and savings all at the same time. More real income, of course, means more spending power in today's dollars. Is a 70 percent median increase absolutely necessary? Would 50 percent be enough? Relatively modest reductions in the *improvement* in senior real incomes could save very large amounts of money. The same research projects that only 7 percent of boomers will have incomes of 150 percent of the poverty line or less in 2030,* disproportionately concentrated, of course, among single people without high school educations. (Even on pessimistic economic assumptions, the number rises to only 11 percent.) True poverty among the aged, therefore, will be very low; most poor people, in fact, will probably be better off after they become eligible for Social Security than before.

• *How to return the Social Security trust fund to long-term actuarial balance.* As we saw in chapter 7, some combination of a relatively small increase in the pay-

*The research cited is a good example of the AARP Personality One and Personality Two in action (see chapter 3). Personality One commissions nonpartisan, nontendentious, high-quality research, and presents it in a factual, let-the-chips-fall-where-they-may manner. But Personality Two always intrudes somewhere to point with alarm. The striking projection that only 7 percent of retired boomers will have incomes at or below 150 percent of the poverty line (plus free medical care), for example, is taken to signal the emergence of "a permanent economic underclass of boomers."

roll tax (perhaps 1 percent), a small adjustment in COLA schedules (.05 percent), a gradual increase in the age of eligibility for full benefits to seventy, and some trimming of benefits to the better-off retirees may well do the trick. (None of this is nearly as radical as the 1983 restructuring.) Refinancing packages should be paired with scenarios for slowing the real growth of income to the aged; that is, How much would it cost to ensure a 70 percent average growth in real incomes—50 percent? 30 percent? The higher the standard of living being financed for tomorrow's seniors, the less justified are payroll taxes on today's workers. Since boomers *are* today's workers, they can hardly complain about trading off lower taxes now for lower average benefits later.

• *A reasonable Social Security benefit skew among retirees.* Because there will be many more affluent retirees than poor ones, relatively mild reductions in benefits to better-off people could fund substantial improvements in the bottom decile. There is probably some limited room for additional redistribution within the Social Security system before the better-off start a clamor for opting out. The question must be approached with caution, however.

• *A sliding-scale earned income exemption to reduce the impact of the "tax" on earned income among retirees.* Over the last thirty years, the country has grown accustomed to a very rapidly growing labor force. But for the next thirty years, the labor force is likely not to grow at all. Even if immigration grows much faster than expected, the number of skilled workers will be quite flat. Skilled seniors, therefore, are likely to be at a premium compared to today. In the 1970s and 1980s, early retirements were good social policy. In the 2020s, we will want to keep people working longer, and will probably be better off by sharing the Social Security savings with them.

• *A tax program for entitlements comparable to that applying to private pension programs*—effectively exempting from taxation only the portion of the benefit representing personal contributions. Personal exemptions would ensure that lower-income seniors were not saddled with taxes.

• *The question of the "surpluses."* As shown in chapter 4, the trust fund surplus calculation ignores the cash flow implications for the federal government when its IOUs are called. My own preference would be to dedicate the current surpluses to the Medicare program, which would put the true cost picture of senior entitlements into better perspective, and will highlight how much sooner the Social Security program will become a cash drain on the federal Treasury.

• *Reform of federal pension benefits.* Despite recent reforms, federal and military pensions are still far higher than any in the private sector, while middle-level federal pay and benefits are now quite competitive. The numbers involved are very large, about $60 billion in 1993, equivalent to half of all private pension payments in the country. The system's COLA provisions are so aggressive that retirees sometimes earn more in retirement than they earned while working.

Whatever the individual package of reforms, the overall goal should be to *incur minimal additional increases in Social Security–related payroll taxes in order to leave funding room for the inevitable spending increases for senior health care.* Ideally, further Social Security–related payroll tax increases should be kept to about the 1 percent level. Given the very large increases in real incomes currently in prospect for retiring boomers, it should be possible to achieve this goal, while more than maintaining the current real value of retirement incomes.

A "Greenspan Commission" is not an essential prerequisite to any of these reforms. It is merely a mechanism for bipartisan cover. In the absence of bipartisan *willingness* to address the issues in a thorough but piecemeal and low-key way, of course, convening a commission will be of no use at all. Nor is there any necessity to produce a single package to be voted up or down, as in the 1983 restructuring or the military-base-closing scenarios. If such a commission is convened, and it proves successful, it should be reconvened at regular intervals, perhaps after every presidential election.

***Health Care*** Reforms in senior health care must be viewed in the context of the overall health care system, which is not the same as saying that only "comprehensive" reform will be meaningful. There are a number of piecemeal reforms that could serve as solid starting points.

• A good place to start would to be to *eliminate the care that people don't want yet is imposed against their express wishes.* A quarter or more of all health care spending, some $250 billion each year, is incurred in the last year of life. There is a growing movement to frame living wills because so many people fear the prolonged indignities of a high-tech death in a modern hospital. Recent studies indicate, however, that up to three quarters of living wills are ignored, for a variety of reasons: hospitals fear malpractice suits, no one knows about the living will, the person designated under the will is not available, doctors just don't listen. A number of steps suggest themselves:

- Create a registry of living wills linked to insurance coverage, so the will travels automatically with the patient's record. Such a project is well within the reach of modern computer technology, probably at a very reasonable cost, considering the amount of money at stake. Pilot projects might be suitable for foundation funding.
- Standardize the legal status of living wills and, if necessary, create safe harbors from malpractice suits by relatives when an institution follows the clear intent of a living will.
- Create a fiduciary in each hospital who can stand in for a missing designated agent when that person is unavailable. Such a fiduciary delegation could be provided for in a newly standardized living will form.

- Under the auspices of the American Medical Association or other body, improve the self-regulation of unwanted or excessive treatment in the last stages of life, with particular emphasis on teaching hospitals, where the temptation to excessive high-technology intervention will be the greatest. Serious attention should be paid to the possibility of developing codified guidelines for end-stage intervention.
- Senior organizations should step up their communications programs on the possibilities and pitfalls of living wills. AARP has already done much good work in this area.

Savings from a more sensible end-of-life treatment protocol could be substantial, simply because end-game medicine now absorbs such a disproportionate share of medical resources.

- A heretical recommendation: *Slow the pace of federal disease-related research*. Yes, more and better health care is a good thing, but new technology is probably arriving faster than the system can absorb it, while the profit motive creates incentives to proliferate treatments that are still of dubious value. The marketing of the Genentech growth hormone to parents of short children and the massive television and newspaper campaign to get men to "ask your doctor" about Proscar, a prostate-reducing drug that is still of questionable efficacy, are recent examples that could be multiplied many times. This is an area that cries out for professional self-regulation, and will almost certainly induce potentially destructive government interventions if the professions fail to police themselves more effectively.

• *Some significant portion of federal disease-related research dollars should be reallocated to more practical, treatment-oriented outcomes and effectiveness studies to develop better protocols and get more mileage out of the technologies we already have.* Suspicious regional treatment patterns should be explored thoroughly—like the tendency of, for example, neurosurgery or bypass surgery to track closely to the number of available neurosurgeons and cardiac surgeons, irrespective of the morbidity characteristics of a service population. We are approaching a day of scarce medical resources and cannot afford to squander what we have so recklessly.

• *We must seriously address the issue of abusive billings.* What is needed at the outset is not more regulation or paperwork, but more information, if only to salvage the reputation of the medical profession. Seniors are the most astute consumers of medical services, and they are convinced that the problem is rampant. Mistrust of the profession is rising to the point where it could become a serious health care issue, and it deserves high-priority research attention. Research cited in chapter 7 suggests that the problem is not large, but the data are poor, and it certainly looms large in the public mind. Serious professional self-regulation will be preferable to more federal regulation, since it will be less likely to create more layers of paperwork.

The fit between the profit motive and health care

is still an uneasy one, because the "consumers" are so vulnerable, and the potential profits so enticing. The worst scandal in recent years may have been the psychiatric hospitals run by National Medical Enterprises. It appears that "bounties" were paid for patients, patients were sedated and held for the maximum time permitted by their insurance, and false billings were rampant. The company pleaded guilty to criminal charges and paid back $379 million. Exploitation of Medicare patients for unneeded medical hardware is apparently widespread. "Upcoding" may be standard practice in some institutions to avoid diagnosis-related fee limits. HMOs are frequently reported as dumping emergency patients on government-supported hospitals. No wonder so many old people hate their doctors. I have no brilliant recommendations, but the situation is awful and the professionals have to take it seriously. Dr. Arnold Relman's 1980 warning in the *New England Journal of Medicine* about the rise of a "medical-industrial complex" is more pertinent than ever.

• *The Republican majority is certainly right to press the spread of managed care programs for Medicare beneficiaries, and should not shrink from the controversial question of limiting physician choice.* Anecdotal reports suggest that doctor-hopping may be rife among seniors. It is expensive, and can even be dangerous, as when drug interactions are poorly monitored. Managed care will doubtless result in some financial savings, but they are likely to be smaller than the congressional majority appears to hope. Seniors will resent the curtailment of physician choice, but Medicare will still remain a superb benefit, worth far more than the actuarial value of lifetime payroll tax payments. Better-off seniors, of course—the majority—will be able to afford out-of-plan treatment in any case if they so choose. Implementing managed care plans is another area where the prevailing distrust of the medical profession is likely to be a problem. Hochstein's focus groups suggest that seniors see the managed care "gatekeeper" physician—the primary care doctor who manages access to specialists—not as an overall care manager but simply as a "sneaky way for two doctors to get paid instead of just one."

• Finally, *we should address the problem of working families without health insurance* by facilitating the creation of no-frills, low-cost major medical policies that cover obstetrics and major illnesses with potentially devastating financial consequences. The Clinton administration's, and AARP's, proposals to achieve universal coverage by mandating a rich level of care for everyone is a classic case of the best as the enemy of the good. Under the pressure of organized service professionals, almost every state has mandated a vast range of minimum requirements for health insurance—alcohol and drug treatment, mental health services, chiropractic—in some states no fewer than thirty-five additional coverages over and above the traditional major medical provisions. Even "no-frills" advocates tend to insist on annual "preventive care" physicals for all plan members, although there is no evidence that healthy younger adults need annual checkups, except for minimal gynecological work like Pap smears.

Where employers still did not provide no-frills coverage, states could create insurance pools so families could purchase it themselves at a group rate. About a quarter of the uninsured, some 10 million people, are single eighteen- to twenty-nine-year-olds. Many would probably still not buy insurance even if the no-frills option were available (but their parents might). The fact that many young singles would still be uncovered would be a problem, but hardly the worst one facing the nation. The point is that substantial improvements in the level of major medical coverage could be achieved without turning the entire health care system upside down, and without large new expenditures of public funds.

***Long-Term Care*** This is one of most serious health care issues facing seniors, but one of the least addressed. It is not a problem that can be solved with a single brilliant stroke, nor are massive new entitlements likely to be forthcoming in the near term. Piecemeal approaches, again, could help considerably.

• It is important to remember that seniors as a group are not poor. Many seniors, of course, are poor, but there are proportionately fewer poor seniors than poor young families or poor children. Seniors control somewhat more than half of all net household wealth, and their share of net wealth is growing rapidly. There is every reason to believe that the next generation of seniors will be even richer than the present one. The first-wave boomer generation, those born before 1955, already has acquired twice the asset value of their parents at a comparable age.

The problem is that senior assets are mostly illiquid. Over-sixty-fives had net assets of more than $1.8 trillion in 1991, but $1.3 trillion was tied up in real estate. Episodes of extended care beyond the period covered by Medicare can have catastrophic cash flow consequences, forcing distress sales of residences by people who are in no position to make clearheaded decisions. Finding nondisruptive ways to liquefy senior real estate assets will be an all-important step toward alleviating the long-term care financing problem. The most promising approach may be standardized, FHA-insured, relatively inexpensive reverse mortgages that allow people to tap the equity value of their homes with repayment assessed against the estate or a subsequent sale. (In a reverse mortgage arrangement, the bank pays the borrower a fixed monthly payment, accumulating a principal liability against the property that grows at a fixed rate of interest.)

Reverse mortgages could easily become a standard way to finance temporary stays in nursing homes, or the care of one spouse, while enabling the other spouse to remain in the couple's home. The FHA has begun pilot experiments with reverse mortgages in several states, but the program would seem to warrant acceleration. "Early" collection against life insurance policies represents another promising approach to liquefy the assets of nominally wealthy but cash-flow-poor seniors.

It may be feasible to create a new class of Medicare financing—for nursing care, or any health care outside the standard Medicare package—with the equivalent of a government-provided home equity line. A senior would incur a service charge from an approved list, the provider would be paid by Medicare "Part C," and a lien would be logged against the estate to accrue interest at the low Treasury rate. The senior out-of-pocket would be limited to any copayments or deductibles that might apply. When the liability rises to some fixed percentage of the available assets, depending on the existence of a spouse, Medicaid could kick in as at present. The only losers under such arrangements are the children of seniors, who may see their inheritances drained away to finance nursing home care, but they do not seem to warrant the highest priority in public sympathies. Indeed, vigilance against asset-shifting in anticipation of long-term-care costs should be raised to an even higher level than at present. AARP, it should be said, is currently doing much useful research and publication in reverse mortgage issues.

• There will need to be a much broader range of care alternatives for the frail and disabled aged, especially less-medicalized forms of custodial care than skilled nursing homes. Home care, hospices, retirement "homes," small-group living, and greatly expanded provision of "life-care" alternatives (settings that provide a graduated range of living alternatives, from independent apartment living to skilled nursing) will all be important. This is an area where states are likely to be much more effective and innovative regulators than the federal government. Centralized regulation of personal services inevitably becomes weighted down with a host of laudable, but frequently irrelevant, professional-interest-group-specific care requirements—in architecture, round-the-clock staffing, credentialing, record-keeping, and many other areas. Costs consequently escalate to the point that the services can be made available only to the lucky few. The Republican proposals for returning Medicaid to the states could generate a wave of long-term-care experimentation, but only if the federal bureaucratic hand is removed from the process. This is also an area in which the AARP Personality Two tends to prevail, recommending rather more, and more centralized, regulation than seems strictly necessary.

• No one has yet cracked the long-term care insurance question. As we saw in chapter 7, the small minority of nursing home cases that extend beyond two years accounts for the lion's share of costs. Insuring against the cost of the two-year-plus stay appears to be economical only if the insurance is purchased relatively early in life, say, by the mid-forties. This may be an area where, for instance, a manageable, but mandated, Part B premium kicking in at an appropriate age would guarantee full nursing home coverage, with only limited recourse to personal assets. If such a premium system were created, the proceeds should be invested by a private-sector insurance pool to avoid the deficit-fudging issues that dog the Social Security "surpluses."

***Other Entitlements*** Seniors are quite right to resent the attention to their entitlements, when they are by no means the most outrageous of government handouts. Peter G. Peterson and his colleagues at the Concord Coalition have stressed the vast range of government subsidies that flow to America's *wealthy*, in the form of direct payments, as in the notorious farm programs and in various business lending programs, and in the form of tax subsidies, like home mortgage interest deductions on very expensive homes. Peterson calculates that in 1991, the average poor family received $5,700 in government benefits, including tax expenditures like the mortgage interest deduction; while the average family with incomes over $100,000 received $9,300 in benefits. Of total subsidies paid in 1991, half flowed to families with incomes in excess of $30,000 and a quarter to families with incomes in excess of $50,000.

The massive American defense budget is a good example. It is shot through with special-interest subsidies. For example, Congress has recently insisted, over the navy's objections, on building more Seawolf-class submarines purely to boost employment in politically sensitive areas of the country. B-2 bombers are another weapon that the Pentagon does not want to buy—it is not clear that the plane really works—but the Congress is insisting on more B-2s, at $2 billion a pop. The fact that America's defense budget is now bigger than the whole rest of the world's combined might prompt some rethinking.

The failure of the new conservative Congress to move aggressively against corporate welfare is truly disappointing. Farmers, it seems, vote Republican, so farm price supports will stay intact, even as they serve to raise the price of food, increase inflation, and aggravate the deficit. Federal subsidies to corporations like McDonald's to advertise their products overseas were *increased* in 1995. Eliminating the space station—the kind of "neat thing that guys like," according to humorist Dave Barry—by itself would be enough to close the near-term deficit in the Medicare trust fund. For all their hawkish deficit posturing, the new Newtoid Republicans have shamefully flunked the pork barrel test, like the Economic Development Administration that funds malls and amusement parks for home districts.

Finally, the deficit-cutting rhetoric and the alarms over Medicare simply do not square with the compulsion to cut taxes. The scheduled tax cuts of $240 billion are roughly equivalent to the scheduled Medicare cuts. All tax cuts, at some level, reduce economic incentives. But it is not so long ago that top tax rates in America were more than double what they are now. In the history of the world, it would be difficult to find another class that has enjoyed such large cuts in tax rates over such a short span of time, but the elusive "incentive to invest" always seems to lie just over the next hill. In any case, given the current boom psychology on Wall Street, it is simply absurd to argue that investment will dry up without further cuts in the capital gains tax.

Cutting corporate welfare and government pork will be of critical importance, partly for financial reasons but more as a symbol of the integrity of the budget-making process. It is perfectly reasonable to recalibrate senior income and health care programs, to trim benefits for the less needy, to ensure that the growth in health care spending is not excessively wasteful. But if seniors are singled out, while the boys in the back room and the silk-suited corporate lobbyists escape unscathed, the process is virtually guaranteed to come unglued.

***Summing Up*** The folly of "comprehensive reform" programs has been one of the mantras of this book. I am rather embarrassed, therefore, to feel compelled to summarize the key recommendations above into a short list of proposals. My defense is that I offer them merely to illustrate that a series of piecemeal reforms can add up to a program that is roughly in the ballpark of what needs to be accomplished.

**1.** We must take for granted that, over time, health care will expand to consume approximately 30 percent of GDP, or twice the present rate of about 15 percent of GDP. That is not a *bad* thing; indeed, it will be vital to generating the jobs and investment to fuel a growing economy.

**2.** If we maintain the current relatively wasteful allocations of health care dollars, 30 percent will certainly not be enough to accommodate all the boomers' perceived health care needs, but it is probably the point where further expansion would run up against impassable bottlenecks. Even if we wanted to spend more on health care at that point, we probably couldn't. Efforts to improve the allocation of resources, like limiting high-tech end-of-life interventions, and introducing new technologies more slowly, with greater attention to efficacy and cost-effectiveness, will therefore be very helpful in getting the most out of the 30 percent. In all likelihood, however, just as with schools, the boomers will have to make do with much less choice, much more queuing, and much more allocation of scarce resources than the present generation of seniors. Such mechanisms will be put into place piecemeal, largely out of necessity. Good planning will help some, but human foresight is not sufficient to come up with complete solutions on paper.

**3.** Since seniors will account for probably two thirds of the additional health care spending, financing mechanisms therefore must be identified that can direct an additional 10 percent of GDP to senior health care.

**4.** In order to preserve room in payroll tax rates to fund the inevitable increases in senior health care costs, the scheduled *growth rate* in Social Security benefits will have to be substantially curtailed. The recommendation here is to target the very large *growth in real income* for the next generation of seniors (which AARP projects at about 70 percent by 2030). Benefit increases targeted for the top half of recipients should be slowed to bring average *real* benefit growth down to the 30 to 50 percent levels, which, coupled with other changes, like extending the age of retirement, could limit required payroll tax increases to about the 1 percent level, and still maintain long-term solvency.

**5.** An additional 6 to 7 percent increase in payroll tax revenues, phased in over the next twenty years (by raising the actual rate and by raising the ceiling of taxable wages), allocated to senior health care would be equivalent to 3 to 4 percent of GDP, depending on how the definition of taxable payrolls is expanded. (Covered payrolls now represent about half of GDP.) Total payroll taxes would then be in the 22 percent range, which is probably the maximum amount sustainable. A 1 to 2 percent income tax surcharge could offset a substantial portion of the required payroll taxes, and would be preferable for tax equity reasons.

6. Roughly half of the remaining amount could be financed by seniors through an orderly and nondisruptive liquidation of real assets, probably through government-insured financings secured by residences or other assets with principal realization deferred until death or the earlier disposition of the asset. Seniors may greatly resent this, but they have very large amounts of locked-up wealth, and there is no other place to go for the money.

7. The remainder could be financed from the government's present resources by dropping current plans for cutting taxes and consciously reallocating defense and non-poverty-related domestic spending toward seniors. To avoid further tax increases, military spending would have to be cut by at least a third, and possibly by half. But, after all, the cold war *is* over. Nobody else in the world is investing in advanced military hardware the way we are, so we should probably just stop. If there is another outbreak of Leninism in Russia, or if some yet-unknown power rises to threaten our safety, we can always gear up the military machine again, and we will make the necessary sacrifices to do so. But there is no reason to make those sacrifices every year in the absence of such a threat. And both parties will have to get serious about pork

and corporate welfare—the farm support payments that go to millionaires, the theme parks that make campaign donors rich, the whole disgraceful list.

One major difference between a health care–oriented economy and the automobile-based economy of the 1950s and 1960s is that car purchases (but not highways) could be financed within the family, at least once installment-credit mechanisms were in place. Health care expenditures, however, can be so massive that risks must be pooled—that is, they must be in some degree socialized, whether the socialization vehicle is a private insurance company or the federal government. The underlying assumption in the proposals above is that the federal government will be the cheapest available vehicle for socializing risk, which will require some expansion of the federal role in the economy. There is no *philosophic* reason why the same result could not be accomplished in a privatized mode, but the mechanisms may have to be so complicated as to be unworkable; in any case, I don't wish to express any inherent bias for one form of solution over another. Even assuming we use the federal government as the primary vehicle, however, the proposals above would still keep the actual federal expansion to a relatively modest level.

Finally, I should like to stress that the proposals are not intended as a Complete Solution, but merely to illustrate that while senior entitlements are a Very Serious Problem, they are not an Overwhelming Crisis, unless we choose to make them so.

* * *

The aging of the baby boomers is the great test facing the American polity over the next thirty years. Our political system is not oriented toward dealing with problems that unfold over such a long period of time. The tendency is to ignore them, or to indulge ourselves in confabulating vast, comprehensive schemes of reform. We must do better than that, and get down to the hard, unglamorous, gritty, piecemeal work of gradually bringing our benefit system into line with our resources, assuring that our vast health care resources are not simply squandered, and maintaining the generational compact with fairness and compassion.

John Quincy Adams was a curmudgeon, given to sour reflections on the fate of the American republic. He once remarked that "Democracy has no forefathers, it looks to no posterity, it is swallowed up in the present and thinks of nothing but itself." The vast demographic transition looming before us is a splendid opportunity to prove him wrong.

# Appendix I

## *The AARP Commercial Empire*

AARP WAS FOUNDED MOSTLY to sell things. The very first page of the very first issue of *Modern Maturity* was a letter from Ethel Percy Andrus extolling the opportunity to buy AARP-sponsored health insurance. Health insurance for older people was a crusade for Andrus, and proved to be the path to riches for Leonard Davis. The Davis/Colonial Penn days are long past, and AARP is no longer merely a marketing machine, as it was when Davis held the reins. Horace Deets insists, with a quiet fervor that is quite convincing, that services and volunteer mobilization are his major priorities. But few people join AARP because they're looking for volunteer opportunities. It's the travel discounts and the AARP products that draw people to cough up the membership fee and entice them into the AARP network. AARP's product-related income was about $183 million in 1994, or about 48 percent of the total, if federal grants are excluded. That percentage has been fairly constant since Davis's day, and since the organization is now so much bigger, the dollar volume of revenue from product sales has grown to levels that probably even Davis dared not dream of. Insurance sales alone (gross sales, not AARP revenue) exceeded $3.5 *billion* in 1994.

Health insurance has always been the mainstay of the AARP product offerings. Unlike its other products, health insurance is sold under the AARP label—as in the AARP Group Hospital Plan, although the plans are underwritten and managed by Prudential Insurance Co. Solicitations are usually on the AARP letterhead and are signed by an AARP official. The rest of the AARP offerings—a growing list of products ranging from mutual funds and annuities to car and homeowners' insurance—are so-called endorsed products. They are marketed by third-party organizations but sport an AARP logo, are listed in the official handbooks and fliers extolling AARP member services, and have access to the advertising pages of *Modern Maturity* and the *AARP Bulletin*. (The two journals do not accept advertising from products that compete directly with AARP-labeled offerings.) In theory, AARP revenues from endorsed products are royalty fees, while the health insurance revenues are payments for administrative services. The distinction may someday be important for calculating AARP's tax liability but is of little relevance to consumers. The table on page 211 lists the major AARP products, along with the number of customers and the revenues accruing to AARP.

According to Wayne Haefer, the official in charge of members' services—AARP-speak for products—AARP tries to craft its offerings to meet needs that are not well served, or not served at all, by competitive products. This was much easier in the early days. For all his flaws, it is to Davis's lasting credit that he

| PRODUCT | MEMBERS* | REVENUES* |
|---|---|---|
| Group Health Insurance | 5.8 million | $119.4 million, including interest |
| Mutual Funds | 800,000 | $7.6 million |
| Pharmacy | 2.5 million | $4.3 million |
| Auto/Home Insurance | 1 million auto<br>600,000 home | $25 million |
| Mobile Home Insurance | 113,000 | $1.7 million |
| Visa/MasterCard | 1.2 million | $8.7 million |
| Motoring Plan | 900,000 | $1.9 million |
| Travel Discounts | c. 10 million | $4.5 million |
| Annuities | New product | NA |
| Life Insurance | New product | NA |

*Members as of end of 1994; 1994 revenues.

blazed the trail for marketing to the elderly. Nobody had sold senior health insurance before Davis did, and he proved that policies could cover a large number of older "lives" and still make money—gobs of it, in fact. He went on to make the same demonstration in the field of auto insurance; most older people, in fact, turned out to be excellent risks. And he was the first to divine that the leisure and discretionary spending power of retirees offered a vast marketing opportunity for travel services and mobile home insurance. It did not take many years for other companies to notice Colonial Penn's high profits, and the field of senior services quickly became a crowded one. The graying of the boomer generation, without doubt one of the great marketing opportunities of the century, has already begun to affect product design. The athletic young people in Levi's ads wear looser-cut jeans than they did a decade ago in deference to spreading boomer waistlines.

The AARP strategy, according to Haefer, is to focus on product niches that are not well covered by commercial companies, or to find a product "spin" that makes it more suitable for older people than competitive offerings. One consistent emphasis is on the accuracy and readability of sales brochures, and the quality of telephone service reps. An informal sampling of the telephone reps suggests that service levels, in fact, are quite good. Calls to a half dozen different AARP-endorsed product vendors were invariably picked up on the second or third ring, and the reps were obviously well trained and knowledgeable. (Mutual fund telephone reps, for example, often have trouble with technical questions on their funds—on the "duration" of a fund, for instance. The AARP/Scudder reps had the information at their fingertips and knew what it meant.) Robert Smith, head of the New York Life Insurance unit offering the AARP life insurance product, says that the AARP oversight is "almost irritating. They're here at least twice a month, they monitor phone calls, and they have a big input into customer service training."

AARP products are not usually the cheapest available. "We're not a discount club," says Haefer, although some products offer excellent values. The major distinguishing characteristic of AARP products is that they offer consistent nationwide pricing schemes, although prices may still vary from state to state, and are typically open to all AARP members, which can be a major advantage for someone who may have difficulty getting insurance or qualifying for a credit card under competitive programs.

Overall, the product offerings are quite creditable, in marked contrast to the Davis years, when AARP products were often the *least* competitive on the market. Even as late as 1988 and 1989, *Consumer Reports* found key AARP insurance offerings "relatively mediocre," and among the "priciest" offerings. The great strides made in recent years, however, make it even more disconcerting to encounter AARP product offerings that are still of dubious value, and the subject of hard-sell marketing besides.

What follows is a brief review of the major AARP products and a rough assessment of their value to members.

## HEALTH INSURANCE

Health insurance is still the flagship AARP product, as it has been since 1958. In pre-Medicare days, AARP sold basic major medical coverage. Once Medicare passed, AARP/Colonial Penn was arguably the first insurance vendor to offer Medicare Supplement, commonly known as Medigap, insurance. Medigap policies are still by far the largest source of AARP product income, accounting for more than 80 percent of health insurance sales and more than half of all AARP product revenue. When the separation from Colonial Penn was engineered in 1981, the health insurance contract was awarded to the Prudential Insurance Co. after intense competition involving a large number of companies, as might be expected given the size of the AARP marketing base. The Prudential has managed the program ever since, although there are regularly established review and renewal dates. The next renewal date arrives in 1997, and in theory at least, the contract could be awarded to another company. Prudential has some 4,000 employees and an extensive physical plant near Philadelphia devoted to its AARP product line. Discussion of rebidding, says Haefer, "tends to raise angst levels quite considerably." About 3 percent of all premium amounts are paid to AARP, along with an interest allowance on the first forty days of premium "float." Total AARP health insurance revenues in 1994, including the interest allowance, was about $120 million.

AARP/Prudential offer four basic programs: Medigap, a hospital supplement plan, a major medical plan, and a long-term care plan.

***Medigap*** Medigap, or Medicare Supplement, policies fill in the interstices of Medicare coverage. They pay the Medicare coinsurance and deductible amounts, which can be substantial, and pick up items like pharmaceuticals and hearing aids that Medicare doesn't pay for. (Under Medicare, seniors must cover the first $716 of hospital care out of their own pockets, and there is a $100 deductible for physician care. In addition, 20 percent copayments apply to a number of Medicare-covered services. To qualify for a Medigap policy, one must have both Part A, for hospitals, and Part B, physician care, as almost all seniors do.)

Medicare is a complicated program, and private insurance companies, following the AARP lead, created hundreds of Medigap policies in the 1970s and 1980s, especially when Medicare deductible and copayment requirements began to climb steadily through the 1980s. In 1990, Congress intervened, and mandated a standard array of ten plans that would be uniform for all companies. The benefit schedules and the core descriptive material are now identical for all plans, so it is easy for a buyer to lay competing offerings side by side and compare one to the other. Plan "F" from the federal menu is the most frequently purchased alternative. (Plan F pays virtually all Medicare copays and deductibles, and picks up costs that exceed Medicare limits, but it does *not* cover pharmaceuticals. The extra coverage for pharmaceuticals in almost all plans, including AARP's, is expensive, requires a qualifying medical examination, and is typically burdened with heavy deductibles, copayments, and annual coverage limits.)

The AARP/Prudential Medigap policies get very high ratings. Debbie Breslin, the bright and brisk director of senior health insurance for the state of New Jersey, says that, for most seniors in New Jersey, the AARP Medigap policy is clearly the best value. *Money* magazine, which periodically rates AARP products, calls the policy "one of the best around."

A comparison of the AARP F plan with the other eight F plan offerings available to seniors in New Jersey offers a good insight into the AARP pricing and product-design strategy:

- The AARP policy's starting monthly premium rate, at $78.75, is roughly at the midpoint of the nine plans, which have a premium range from \$63.17 to \$97.25.

- But the AARP premium is the only one that is not adjusted for the beneficiary's age. All other quoted premiums are for 65-year-olds, and increase with the age of the beneficiary. For people in their 70s, the AARP policy would almost always have the lowest price.
- All but one of the other policies required a health examination before accepting an application for coverage. The AARP policy did not; members are automatically eligible. (But AARP requires a medical screening for the higher-end policies that cover pharmaceuticals, as did all of the other policies.)
- Two plans had no waiting period before coverage took effect, compared to AARP's 90-day period. The other plans all had 90- or 180-day waiting periods. The AARP waiting period was waived if the coverage was applied for at the same time the beneficiary became eligible for Medicare.
- Finally, according to Breslin, the AARP policies had an excellent reputation for claims handling and dispute resolution.

The AARP Medigap benefit ratio, the percentage of revenue that is paid out in claims, is quite high. Federal law mandates a minimum benefit ratio of 75 percent, while the AARP contract with Prudential sets a minimum of 78 percent. In the recent past, the actual AARP benefit ratio has been in the 86 to 88 percent range, which is excellent. (In the 1970s, the Colonial Penn benefit ratio hovered around 63 percent, and occasionally dipped to the low 50s.) In 1993,

Prudential refunded portions of premium payments when claims payment experience produced a benefit ratio lower than that year's target of 88 percent.

Insurance is a volume-sensitive business. Centralized mailing and claims processing offers economies of scale that permit profitable operations at high levels of benefit payouts. With some 3 million lives, AARP is second only to Blue Cross in numbers of Medigap beneficiaries, and the Blues are really a loose confederation of separate companies rather than a single provider.

Haefer believes that the AARP policies are the only ones that offer all ten federal plans in every state, and within each state, pricing is uniform for all AARP members. With the exception of the pharmaceutical policies, all AARP members are automatically eligible without a physical examination, and no individual can be dropped because of a claims history. Price-conscious seniors in good physical health will usually be able to find a lower-cost policy during their first years of retirement, but as they grow older, their age-adjusted premiums will rise to a point that they will almost always do better with an AARP policy. A very large policy base, coupled with highly cost-efficient marketing—Prudential advertises its AARP policies only in the pages of *Modern Maturity*—has been parlayed into a solid value for members, which is pretty much what AARP was always supposed to be about.

***Hospital Supplements*** Hospital supplements are the second-most-popular AARP product, with some 2.7 million policies. Since premiums and benefits are much lower than for Medigap, however, the policies are a much less important component of AARP revenues. AARP's policies were severely criticized in the most recent *Money* magazine survey—"No matter how old you are, stay away"—and rightly so. But the criticism more accurately applies to the very concept of hospital supplement insurance rather than specifically to AARP's policies, which are quite a bit better than most. Still, it is lousy insurance, and it raises the question of AARP's duties to its members: As a member services organization, is it supposed to sell them what they want, or train them to be better insurance consumers?

Hospital supplement policies pay small levels of benefits, usually $60 to $120 a day for each day in the hospital, in return for relatively low premiums. The AARP premiums, depending on the plan, range from $13.50 to $27 a month. The problem is that paying small premiums for small benefits with frequent payouts violates basic insurance principles. Insurance is most cost-effective when large numbers of people pool their premiums to protect themselves against infrequent, unpredictable, catastrophic events. Life insurance is a good example. The odds that a young family head will die unexpectedly may be very low, but if she should, the consequences would be disastrous. Merely putting life insurance premiums in the bank could never provide the required protection against catastrophe; it is the disaster protection features of life insurance and major medical policies that make them sensible propositions, even though their actual financial returns are low. But when no catastrophe is being insured against, when small premiums are merely being paid back in small benefits, as in hospital supplement policies, the cost of administering the insurance pool eats up the value of the insurance, and the insured would almost always be better off simply plunking the premium into a bank account.

Hospital supplement policies are wildly popular, however, because they pay *cash* directly to the beneficiary. New Jersey's Breslin throws up her hands at hospital supplement policies. "I was helping an older friend who'd been ill get her paperwork in order," she says, "and she told me to file the claim for her supplement policy first because she had $150 coming to her. I said, 'A hundred and fifty dollars! You've been paying into this policy for ten or twelve years. You've spent more than a thousand dollars. You should have just put it in the bank.' She said, 'But I wouldn't have *put* it in the bank, and now I have cash coming to me that I can use for whatever I want.'" Collecting on a supplement policy, in short, feels like found money. The unexpected cash takes a little edge off being sick, and, however uneconomic the policies may be as financial propositions, consumers like them.

In the matter of hospital supplements, therefore, AARP has chosen to go with the flow—since so many of their members will buy supplement policies anyway, they may as well offer them a relatively good one. Bill Matusz, the head of the Prudential AARP insurance operation, says that the benefit payout ratio is about 80 percent of premiums, or far higher than the average in the industry. Susan Polniaszek, a fee-based insurance consultant (meaning she doesn't sell policies) who specializes in consumer issues, says it is not uncommon to see benefit ratios as low as 30 to

50 percent in competing products. In addition, the marketing materials are clearly written and take pains to emphasize that the supplement policy is not a substitute for basic hospital insurance, a frequent source of confusion among policy buyers not yet eligible for Medicare.

Polniaszek, however, laments that AARP has chosen to offer the product at all. "They're passing up a great consumer education opportunity," she says. "They should be educating their members *not* to buy this stuff." Even if AARP is justified in *offering* the product, however, its marketing campaign seems extremely aggressive given the policy's uneconomic nature. When a new member joins AARP, virtually the first contact with the organization is a packet containing an insurance card that could easily be confused with the AARP membership card, along with a "Guaranteed Enrollment Certificate" and a personalized note from executive director Horace Deets: "We would like to extend our warmest 'welcome' on the occasion of your becoming an AARP member. And we would like to remind you that you may now enroll for one of the most valued benefits of membership—easy-to-obtain [hospital supplement] insurance." Failure to respond draws almost weekly additional mailings extolling the wonderful opportunity that the new member is passing up. Taken together, it is the hardest sell for any AARP product and, given its dubious value, a bit unseemly.

***Major Medical and Long-Term Care*** The last two AARP/Prudential offerings are small programs with relatively little revenue impact.

The major medical policy provides primarily hospital benefits for uninsured members not yet eligible for Medicare. A decade or so ago, a self-employed or temporarily unemployed person could readily purchase a major medical policy geared to catastrophic medical episodes (there was usually a high deductible and high copayments up to an annual ceiling) for relatively low premiums. It was a cost-effective way to buy peace of mind, which is what insurance is for. Almost all mainline companies have since withdrawn their offerings, so the AARP product fills a real need—consider the plight of the downsized fifty-five-year-old who has lost his company coverage—and appears to be quite reasonably priced. The pity is only that state regulatory barriers prevent its being offered everywhere in the country.

The long-term care policy, to cover nursing home care, was recently criticized by *Money* magazine for high premium rates and restrictive coverage. Prudential's Matusz concedes that Prudential may not know *how* to price the policy, because of its "very long tail." Prudential has offered the product for ten years, but has only 70,000 enrollees. "The average age of our insureds," says Matusz, "is 65 or 66. But the average age for entering a nursing home is 81, so we have almost no experience to base our rates on." Prudential has also concluded that it is difficult to sell nursing home insurance through the mail, since the very notion is so repellent to most people. This particular program, which may represent a failed experiment, is probably more suggestive of the difficulty of devising broadly acceptable nursing home coverage plans than of special failings on the part of AARP or Prudential.

# MUTUAL FUNDS

AARP members are invited to invest in nine AARP-sponsored mutual funds, managed by Scudder, Stevens, Clark, Inc., a large mutual fund company that distributes its products through stockbrokers, banks, and financial planners, and by direct sales over the telephone. Scudder has managed the AARP mutual funds since the product was first introduced in 1985. As of mid-1995, the eight AARP/Scudder funds had $11.9 billion under management, paying almost $8 million in fees to AARP. The fee is on a sliding scale that currently yields about .065 percent of funds under management—that is, each year about 65 cents of every $1,000 that AARP members have invested in Scudder funds is deducted from their accounts and paid to AARP. By mutual fund industry standards, the AARP royalty fee is not high, and compares favorably with the sales fees extracted by banks and brokerage firms for funds they distribute.

AARP entered the mutual fund business because their surveys showed that their members were curious about funds, had money to invest, but too often had no idea how to select a fund. AARP's objective, therefore, was to set up a series of reasonably priced, low-risk funds, especially adapted to the investment needs of older people, who would likely be making their first mutual fund investment. Much attention has been devoted to producing clear and readable marketing materials, and training telephone reps to be responsive and patient. On user-friendliness, a primary AARP objective, the AARP/Scudder funds score high. The telephone service seems particularly good. The disclosure materials, while not without flaws, are far better than the industry standard. Initial investment requirements, at only $500, are quite low. Management fees and other charges are not the lowest in the industry, but they are certainly competitive, and are much lower than the charges typically imposed by funds sold by banks and brokerage houses. There are none of the sales loads or "12b-1 fees" (trailing sales charges) that drive up expenses in many other fund families.

The problem is that as a group, although there have been one or two excellent performers, the AARP/Scudder funds offer a rather lackluster set of investment options. The bond funds, in particular, have been quite volatile in the recent past—that is, they have been precisely the kind of investment that an older person, who is interested in preserving her assets, should *not* be putting her money into. The Insured Tax-Free General [Municipal] Bond Fund, for example—nothing could sound safer—*lost* 6.22 percent of its value in 1994. So, if you started with $1,000, you ended the year with $937.80. The High-Quality Bond Fund lost 4.48 percent. Nineteen ninety-four was a difficult year for bonds, and the average bond fund lost 2.92 percent. But the AARP/Scudder tax-free fund was down more than twice as much as the average, and the "high-quality" fund was down about 50 percent more than the average. (All performance data in this section are from the Morningstar mutual fund reporting service.) The extra volatility was not just a matter of bad luck but was inherent in the investment strategy chosen for the funds.

***Risk and Bonds*** Relatively few investors truly understand the risks in bond investing. Part of the problem stems from bond salesmen on radio and television hawking the advantages of "safe" tax-free municipal bonds. High-grade municipal bonds and U.S. Treasury bonds are, indeed, "safe" in the sense that they will pay off the face value of the bond when it is due (despite the occasional Orange County–type fiasco). In this respect, they are much safer than, say, low-grade corporate bonds, where the risk of default can be serious. But default is only *one* source of risk in bond investing, and in the case of longer-term bonds not at all the most important one.

Suppose you hold a bond with a face value of $100, paying $5 per year interest, that was newly issued by the U.S. Treasury with a maturity of thirty years. The bond is essentially a contract to pay you $5 every year for 30 years and then pay back your $100 when the 30 years are up. There is no risk at all that the government will default on its $5 annual payment or on the $100 payment 30 years from now.

But suppose you need cash and want to sell your bond. How much will it be worth? The answer depends on what interest rates are doing. When you paid $100 for a bond with a $5 annual interest coupon, the long-term risk-free interest rate, presumably, was 5 percent. Now suppose interest rates go up to 10 percent. Your contract with the government will not change; Uncle Sam will still be obliged to pay you only $5 per year. But if long-term interest rates are 10 percent, a contract to pay $5 per year is worth only $50. The value of your investment has been cut in *half*! (The obligation to repay the $100 is of almost no effect. At an annual inflation rate of 3 percent, the right to collect $100 in 30 years is worth close to nothing.) The opposite will happen if interest rates fall; long-term bonds shoot up in value. The first principle of bond investing is that when interest rates *rise*, the value of the bonds in your portfolio will *fall*. Conversely, when interest rates fall, the value of the bonds in your portfolio will *rise*. In short, there can be quite dramatic fluctuations in bond values for reasons quite unrelated to the creditworthiness of the borrower.

The second basic principle is that *long-term* bonds will be much more volatile than short-term bonds. (Suppose you buy a one-year $100 Treasury issue with a $5 coupon. Since you will get your money back with interest in a year, it is the repayment of the $100, the principal amount, that dominates the cash flows. So in the case of *short-term* bonds, even if rates go up a lot, the value of the bond won't change much.) Finally, *municipal* bonds, because they generally have very long maturities,* tend to be the most volatile bonds of all. Long-term bonds, of course, pay higher interest rates to compensate for the additional risk. If one intends never to sell the bond, but merely to collect interest, the market fluctuations are irrelevant.

*In general, the longer cash flows stretch out, the more volatile the bond. Municipal bonds usually pay lower interest rates than U.S. Treasury bonds, since they are tax-free, so there is less up-front cash flow (or, which amounts to the same thing, the cash flow is more back-end-loaded toward the principal payment). Given a Treasury bond and a high-grade municipal bond of the same maturity, therefore, the value of the municipal bond will be the more volatile with respect to changes in the interest rate, and therefore the riskier investment. It takes rather complicated calculations to decide whether the extra volatility is offset by the tax break.

But for the unsophisticated investor, who may need to get hold of her money, the little extra interest rate kick is almost never worth the risk of big price swings.

The last thing that an older person, having made his very first mutual fund investment in an AARP-recommended "high-quality" bond fund, will expect to see is his principal drop in value. AARP's own surveys show that their investors "hate to see their funds swinging around wildly." It is therefore something of a mystery why the AARP/Scudder bond funds are distinctly weighted toward the long (i.e., most volatile) end of the spectrum. Besides the two funds mentioned, there is one other bond fund, the GNMA & U.S. Treasury fund, that has had rather better performance and has been much less volatile than the other two funds. But even this fund was rated "Mediocre" by Morningstar in late 1994 in terms of asset protection, although it now seems much improved.

Finally, although the disclosure materials for the AARP/Scudder funds were generally very good, they did not point specifically at the price-fluctuation risk in their bond funds. By contrast, the Vanguard fund family, which is the gold standard for low-cost, conservatively managed mutual fund investing, provides a table for each of its bond funds that shows precisely how much the portfolio's value will drop for each 1 percent increase in interest rates. Reportedly, as of mid-1995, the AARP/Scudder funds are restructuring their portfolios to reduce their volatility. The GNMA & U.S. Treasury fund, at any rate, is now *less* volatile than the bond market average, which is a much-needed revision, but the other two funds are still saddled with above-average volatility.

***Equity (Stock) Funds*** AARP/Scudder offer two major stock funds, a Growth and Income fund, which has been the star of the show, and a Capital Growth fund, which has been a dog. In 1995, a Balanced Fund was added to the mix, combining both stocks and bonds, and will be managed by the Growth and Income team. At this writing, its track record is too short to be meaningful. Before commenting on these particular funds, however, a few remarks on the generic problem of equity mutual fund investing are in order.

Over the long term, stocks have been excellent investments. On average, since 1926, stocks have returned about 10 percent a year, or about twice as much as bonds, and considerably more than savings accounts. But stocks are more volatile than most other investments, with bigger up and down swings. Any money you may need in a hurry, therefore, should not be in stocks because you may be forced to sell on a downturn. A good rule is to invest in stocks only when you can safely plan to leave your money alone for three to five years. (Downturns longer than that are very rare.) Just as your short-term savings don't belong in stocks, it is foolish to let your long-term savings languish in money market funds or savings accounts. A $1,000 investment that returns 10 percent a year will be worth about $2,600 in ten years. At 5 percent, it will be worth only $1,600.

The next question is: Can your stock fund "beat the market"?—that is, earn the "superior returns" that all fund managers promise. Twenty years or so ago, that was not such an idle promise. Most stock market trading was done by individuals—the proverbial Aunt Tillie and Uncle Harry, who traded on tips from their brother-in-law—and professionals could count on beating the market most of the time. (But statistics to prove it are sparse.)

But Harry and Tillie are no longer a factor in modern markets, because almost all trading is done by professionals trading for pension funds, insurance companies, and mutual funds. In an electronic era, any trader has essentially the same information as any other. Professional traders now *are* the market. While they still might out-trade Uncle Harry, it is unreasonable to believe, on average, that they can beat the market, which is, after all, just themselves. Academic theory would predict that about half of all fund managers will beat the market in any year and half will fall short, and the distribution of winners and losers will be somewhat random from year to year.

The test of the theory is so-called index investing. Index investors don't try to beat the stock market at all, and they don't hire expensive managers to pick and choose the perfect stock. Instead, they buy a mix of stocks that represents the entire market. The usual proxy for the market is the Standard and Poor's 500 Composite Stock Price Index (the S&P 500), which includes all the largest stocks and accounts for about 70 percent of the stock market's total value. The first, and still the best-known, index fund available to retail investors is Vanguard's 500 Index Trust, designed to match the S&P 500. From 1980 to 1995, it has outperformed the average actively managed equity fund in 11 of the 15 years, outperforming 7 out of 10 actively managed funds over the entire period, and 8 out of 10 since 1985. For what it's worth, Leonard Davis's Florida foundation invests in the Vanguard Index Trust, but not in AARP funds.

There are very few striking exceptions to the rule that active managers can't consistently beat the market, like Fidelity's famous Magellan Fund. It is entirely possible that the market *follows* certain funds. If the whole world buys whatever I buy, I will always outperform the rest of the world, since I bought first and subsequent buyers will simply push up the price. Something like that may explain the Magellan results. On the other hand, sheer chance would also predict that a *few* active managers will beat the market over a long period.

The few exceptions aside, however, the success of index investing exposes the emptiness of the average fund manager's claim that he will outperform the market. In fact, most active managers do considerably *worse* than the market, for the obvious reasons that they tend to trade a lot, which is expensive, and they charge fees, which detracts from their performance. An index fund, for the most part, sells stock only when a company falls out of the index and must be replaced by another stock. Costs are therefore low, and Vanguard's fees are the lowest in the business—a third to a fifth that charged by managed funds. In addition, since there is minimal trading, indexed funds are *tax efficient* because they are not constantly generating capital gains.

About the only times that active managers consistently beat the index funds is in down markets. Index funds, by definition, stay fully invested in stocks, while active managers can park their money in cash until the downturn ends. But the market rises much more often than it falls, and the long-term investor, who plans to leave his money in over the entire market cycle, is usually better off sitting in an index fund. Some of the canniest investors, like the massive California state pension fund, the largest investor in the country, have been steadily moving their equity holdings into indexed investments for a considerable period.

That context is helpful for reviewing the performance of the two main AARP/Scudder equity funds. The Growth and Income fund has been simply outstanding. Its mix of stocks is chosen to be somewhat *less* volatile than the market average and, remarkably enough, it is one of the very few funds that managed to beat the S&P 500 index for three straight years—from 1992 through 1994. (Like almost all funds, it is lagging the index by a good margin through the first half of 1995.) All in all, it has been an excellent run, and it has been rewarded by being the favorite AARP investment, with almost half of the assets under management. It will be interesting to see how long the management team can keep it up; theory, at least, predicts that they should slip back to the mean. The Capital Growth fund, on the other hand, after good performance in 1991 and 1993, suffered a terrible 1994, losing more than 10 percent of its value. A new management team is in place and has performed well through the first half of 1995, although they also lag the S&P 500 index.

Finally, AARP/Scudder offer two conventional money market funds. *Money* magazine criticized them for showing slightly lower returns than the average, but that is often a *good* sign in money market funds, suggesting conservative management. In recent years, in their zeal to capture that elusive extra half-point of yield, many fund managers have been tempted into undue risks. The expense ratios of the AARP/Scudder funds, on the other hand, at 0.96 percent, seem a bit on the high side.

In summary, the record of the AARP/Scudder funds is spotty at best. About half the funds represent investments that are simply badly suited to people whose first concern must be asset-preservation, which is inexcusable. AARP and Scudder are clearly trying to repair the more volatile funds, but even if the poor performers get better, the question is whether any small subset of actively managed funds can *ever* represent themselves as the best choice for AARP members. It is interesting in this regard that almost no other large membership organization has been successful in creating "affinity" mutual fund families, although many have tried. The problem may be in the concept as much as in the execution. With some 6,000 funds on the market, it is not at all obvious why AARP brings anything special to the table. Many funds charge high fees, of course, or are unsuitable for older investors, or have poor disclosure material. But there are others, like the Vanguard family, that arguably beat the AARP/Scudder offerings in all these respects, and offer a much wider range of choices.

The obvious question is why not simply identify fund families that meet AARP standards of suitability and excellence, and allow them to advertise in *Modern Maturity*, or otherwise give them an AARP seal of approval. Haefer responds, a bit stubbornly perhaps, that AARP is not a "Consumers' Union." It is a membership service organization whose job is to provide services, not consumer advice. It seems a flimsy rationalization. The automatic eligibility feature that justifies AARP's insurance offerings doesn't apply to mutual funds. And it leaves AARP open to the charge that they are in the funds business just to make money.

## OTHER PRODUCTS AND SERVICES

### *Insurance Products*

AARP insurance products are generally good buys. As with all AARP products, there is a trade-off between AARP's strategy of providing relatively uniform coverage and eligibility criteria for all of its members and providing the best policy value for people who are good risks. An older person who may have trouble getting insurance from other vendors will usually find that the AARP policies offer the best deal on the market. For younger members, or members in good risk groups, it is advisable to shop first, but the AARP policies are still often good values.

***Home Insurance*** Vic Pizzolato, a Long Island AARP chapter president, ran an insurance brokerage before he retired, and still sells homeowners' insurance part-time. He says he recently switched his own homeowners' policy to AARP (offered through ITT Hartford) because it was the best deal he could find.

The *Money* magazine survey also rated the AARP/ITT Hartford offering very highly.

AARP also offers mobile home insurance, in conjunction with Foremost Insurance Co. The policies have always been considered good values, and in the wake of recent storm devastations, the commitment to offering uniform coverage is serving members well. Haefer admits to some discomfort that AARP/Foremost, as of mid-1995, was the *only* company writing mobile home policies in the state of Florida.

***Automobile Insurance*** As much as any other AARP product, the AARP/ITT Hartford auto insurance policy may require shopping around. Automobile insurance costs and policy regulations vary widely from state to state, and Haefer concedes that his lowest-common-denominator pricing policy may make the AARP policies uncompetitive for, say, 70-year-olds who drive to work every day. In comparisons with two other large low-cost insurers in three hypothetical cases, *Money* magazine found the AARP policy was the cheapest in one case and the most expensive in one other. Even when they are not the best buys, however, members should usually find that the AARP/ITT Hartford policies are in the lower-cost tier.

***Life Insurance*** AARP began to offer life insurance in 1995 in conjunction with New York Life. The policies have been harshly criticized by, among others, Peter Katt, a fee-based insurance consultant in Kalamazoo, Michigan. Like the hospital supplement policies, the life policies suffer from being oriented toward small face values—$25,000 is the maximum benefit, so the cost of administration eats up policy values. In addition, the uniform pricing policy makes them very expensive for people who are good risks. The person who gets the best value from an AARP/New York Life policy, says Katt, is "a smoking male."

But Robert Smith, the responsible New York Life executive, makes a convincing case that the policies are giving members what they want. New York Life competed with 30 other companies for the contract, conducted a number of focus groups with AARP members, and designed the coverage that AARP's surveys and members themselves said they wanted. The policies will be sold to any AARP member up to age 80, and will stay in force up to age 100. None of them requires a physical. Any AARP member, regardless of his health, is eligible for the "Guaranteed Acceptance" policy, although benefits are reduced if death occurs within the first two years. The other policy applications contain either three or four health-related questions (e.g., Do you have AIDS? or Have you consulted a doctor for a heart condition or cancer?). As with all AARP insurance, once a member is insured, she cannot be dropped.

It is conventional wisdom among insurance experts that most older people don't need life insurance, and that low-face-value insurance is intrinsically uneconomic. On the other hand, AARP members clearly want this kind of coverage, and it would be hard to buy similar policies anywhere else, especially for the poorer risks. Initial sales, in fact, have been skewed even more than expected toward the lower face values. Since the premiums are "community-rated"—that is, all people the same age are treated alike—people who are good risks can almost certainly find better buys. The life insurance policies, therefore, are much like the hospital supplement policy. On strict insurance principles, you should talk your grandmother out of buying them; but if she insists on it, the policies are clearly not rip-offs and, depending on her age and health, may be the very best she can get.

### *Financial Products*

***Bank Cards*** "Affinity" bank cards are now an established part of the American financial landscape. Most large membership organizations offer cards, and in many cities, you can get a VISA or MasterCard with the logo of your favorite sports team. The AARP cards are offered through Ohio's BancOne, one of the premier card-processing companies. They have no annual fees, and interest rates are lower than most, although not the very lowest available. AARP's royalty fees are based on a percentage of BancOne's earnings above a threshold. The royalty system causes a slight twinge, because it means that AARP gets paid more if its members borrow more, and bank card borrowing is expensive. But it doesn't appear that AARP actually encourages its members to borrow. Since all members are automatically eligible, the cards will be very attractive for people who have trouble establishing credit, which could include both people with bad credit histories or newly widowed women whose finances were controlled by their husbands.

***Annuities*** The AARP annuities are a new offering, established in 1995. They are sold in conjunction with an insurance joint venture owned by ITT Hartford and Pacific Mutual Life. Annuities may be an ideal AARP product. It is an area of much consumer confusion and misleading marketing. Annuities lend themselves to a variety of exotic structures appropriate for, say, executive benefit programs but not for the average AARP member, and heavy sales commissions can eat into the value of annuities sold by many insurance companies. AARP's initial product offerings are straightforward and safe, and there are no sales commissions. The investment policy quite explicitly trades off higher returns for principal protection, which seems altogether appropriate. Taken together, the annuities are a good addition to the AARP portfolio.

### *Other Products and Services*

***Mail-Order Pharmaceuticals*** RPS, Inc. (Retired Persons' Services), a nonprofit, taxable, privately held company, was one of the very first service operations set up by Andrus and Davis after the founding of AARP, but it was never part of the Colonial Penn empire. It is technically not under the control of AARP, although four of the eight directors are AARP appointees, and its sole business is the provision of mail-order pharmaceuticals to AARP members. It was one of the very first mail-order pharmaceutical services, and it is still one of the few that is not tied to a health care network. Other networks will beat it on price for this or that drug, but overall, it offers good value and excellent service, and has contributed to making life much tougher for your neighborhood druggist.

***Automobile Club*** In conjunction with the Amoco Motoring Club, the AARP Motor Club offers a conventional road service. Its pricing and services are comparable to other service clubs, but it has a smaller network than the giant AAA.

***Travel Discounts*** A third of AARP members take advantage of lodging discounts, like those at Holiday Inn and Marriott, and 5 percent use the discount auto rental programs offered by Hertz and Avis. AARP deserves credit for pioneering senior discounting, but it is now widespread in the hospitality industry, and seniors with business or other affiliations can often match or beat the AARP discounts. Oldsters without other connections who travel infrequently, however, value the AARP discounts highly. Hertz and Avis pay a 5 percent royalty to AARP whenever someone uses an AARP discount. The hotel chains are also mentioned in AARP membership material but don't pay royalties. Although the travel discounts are only a minuscule part of the overall AARP operation, they are still the primary reason why people keep stumping up the annual membership fee. For many years, AARP also offered a travel booking and charter tour service, but that was discontinued in 1995 for lack of business.

## TAXES AND POSTAL FEES

In 1993, AARP settled a long-standing dispute with the Internal Revenue Service by making an "in lieu of" tax payment of $135 million covering the tax years 1985 through 1993. AARP also agreed to make an annual $15 million "in lieu of" tax payment in 1994 and presumably will continue to do so. Strictly speaking, the "in lieu of" settlement represented neither an assessment of tax liability by the IRS nor an admission of liability by AARP. Although the books are closed on the past, the IRS could pursue its inquiry in the future. The expectation, however, is that so long as the voluntary payments continue in the same proportion to product revenues, the IRS will be satisfied. Also in 1993, AARP made a $2.8 million payment to the Post Office to settle another long-standing dispute over the use of its nonprofit mailing privilege for product solicitations. The dispute with the Post Office came in for special criticism at the Simpson hearings.

The fact that AARP could "write a check" to cover such large payments understandably raised eyebrows. In truth, AARP had been marshaling its assets for some time in anticipation of a settlement, and the payment imposed some real strain on its balance sheet. But the fact that such large outlays could be covered without borrowing is indicative of the organization's great financial strength.

The issues involved in the tax and postal disputes are complicated. AARP is a so-called 501(c)(4) organization, after the section of the tax code that provides tax-exemption for organizations engaged in the "promotion of social welfare"; 501(c)(4) organizations are not permitted to participate in political campaigns on behalf of political candidates, but they are permitted to "influence legislation by propaganda" or other means. (AARP, in principle, could legally organize a separate political action committee, or PAC, to support individual candidates but has chosen not to do so.) The code also provides that if an exempt organization derives income from an "unrelated trade or business activity" that income *is* taxable. As might be expected, the determination of what is "related" or "unrelated" business income has been a rich source of dispute between the IRS and tax-exempt organizations. (For example, the IRS has always treated income from on-site museum stores as tax-exempt, but is inclined to fight over sales from satellite stores.)

The dispute over the tax status of AARP revenues involves several quite different issues.

- AARP has never disputed that revenues from financial services and advertising constitute taxable "unrelated" business income. AARP paid $5.8 million in taxes on its financial services revenues in 1994. (This is in addition to the "in lieu of" payment.) It concedes as well that it would owe taxes on advertising revenue from *Modern Maturity* and other publications if they made a profit, but they currently incur large losses.
- AARP also concedes that all the other non–health insurance businesses are "unrelated" business. But income from *royalty fees* for the use of an exempt organization's name are an exception to the "unrelated" rule and are nontaxable. The IRS claims that the income that AARP calls "royalties" are really proceeds from selling *mailing lists*, and therefore taxable, while AARP argues that they fall under the royalty exclusion. Legions of lawyers could wax fat while that one is decided.
- Finally, with respect to health insurance, AARP

> contends that it is a *related* business activity, one that has been a central purpose of the organization since its founding, and thus produces exempt income. Over the years, however, the definition of related product income has been tightened so it applies only to income from products that are not otherwise commercially available. AARP argues that it *still* meets the definition because the automatic eligibility feature of its insurance is unique. The IRS contends that that is not sufficient to meet the test.

None of the AARP arguments is frivolous, although the IRS case also seems strong, particularly with regard to the health insurance. Tax court outcomes, however, are never knowable in advance, and a settlement clearly seems to have been in the interest of both sides. The negative publicity alone was potentially very costly to AARP. Neither AARP nor the IRS have disclosed the details of the settlement, and the dispute officially remains open. Making a rough estimate of the deductible expenses that AARP might attribute to its product revenues suggests that AARP's "in lieu of" payment represents about half the normal corporate tax rate. In short, AARP and the IRS may have split their differences.

Senator Alan Simpson quite properly raises the question of why Congress should *ever* exempt such large amounts of revenues from taxation: Why should nonprofit organizations be allowed to compete with private industry on a tax-favored basis? Simpson and his staff originally planned to propose legislation to limit the nontaxable business income of exempt organizations to, say, 20 percent of their total income, which seems reasonable, and also should be high enough to protect museums and libraries. As of this writing, however, they have contented themselves with proposing tightening the law on lobbying by organizations that receive federal grants. One of the more shocking revelations of the Simpson hearings, in fact, was that there are more than a million 501(c)(4) organizations, and, on average, *90 percent* of their income is from business activities, which makes AARP look good. The AARP board, according to Deets, has set a target of deriving more than half of their income, excluding federal grants, from membership dues. Dues revenues amounted to 38 percent of the total in 1994.

The process by which AARP settled its outstanding dispute with the postal service was also severely criticized at the Simpson hearings. In its earlier days, there seems to be little doubt that AARP abused its nonprofit mailing status. Over the years, the Post Office tightened its regulations to bring more and more of the AARP mailings under business mailing rates. Recent legislation clearly brought virtually *all* of AARP's product-related mailings under business rates. Instead of immediately complying, AARP proposed to the Post Office that they cooperate in submitting amending legislation. The Post Office did not go along, and issued a preliminary rule-making incorporating the new legislation, which was made final six months later. AARP contested the preliminary rule-making, but paid the back postage rates under the new rules when they were made final. Simpson's criticism was that they should have complied immediately.

AARP clearly behaved within the law, but Simpson's criticisms are well founded. Especially given its past, and its very large income, AARP's taking a stand on technical grounds to maintain preferential postal treatment is insensitive to say the least, and invites hostile sallies by its critics. AARP's counsel, Steve Zaleznick, says that all current product-related mailings go at standard business rates. A blended rate applies to publications reflecting the portion that is advertising material.

## SUMMARY

The settlements with the IRS and the Post Office go far to clean up the last detritus from the Davis years. Overall, the AARP product list, like Medigap, the annuities, and even the much-criticized life insurance, offer prices and services that the less advantaged and less sophisticated AARP member would find hard to match, and some would find impossible to purchase at any price. The fact that younger or healthier AARP members can often find better deals doesn't detract from the products' value. Finding the best price for every member would be impossible in any case. There is still the occasional instance of hard-selling a more dubious product, like the hospital supplement policies, that makes a friendly critic cringe. And, in the case of mutual funds, the AARP offering falls well short of its objective and might better be simply dropped. But overall, the member offerings are a respectable show and represent dramatic progress from the disgraceful profit-mongering of AARP's first two decades.

# Appendix II

## *Social Security and Medicare/Medicaid*

### SOCIAL SECURITY

THE SOCIAL SECURITY ACT is intended to provide a retirement income to workers, as well as provide income to workers who became disabled or to their families in the event of the worker's death. This section focuses primarily on the rules concerning Social Security retirement, and not disability and survivor (death) benefits.

#### *Coverage*

The original Social Security Act of 1935 covered employees in nonagricultural and commerce jobs. Since then, coverage has been extended to include most employment, and approximately 96 percent of the jobs in this country are covered under the program. Those who are excluded from coverage are primarily from the following groups:

- Federal civilian employees hired before January 1984
- Railroad workers (covered under the railroad retirement system, coordinated with Social Security)
- Certain state and local government employees who are covered under a retirement system
- Household workers and farm workers whose earnings do not meet minimum requirements
- Persons with very low net income (less than $400 per year) from self-employment

Work performed in the country (including U.S. possessions) is covered by the program regardless of citizenship status of the employee. In addition, the program also covers work performed outside the U.S. by American citizens or resident aliens who (1) are employed by an American company, (2) work for an American affiliate of a company that opts to cover its employees, or (3) are self-employed, under certain circumstances.

### *No Means Test*

Social Security benefits are a right and are paid to eligible retirees regardless of income from other sources (e.g., pensions, savings, nonwork income).

### *Benefit Eligibility*

In order to qualify to receive benefits, including payments for eligible family members and survivors, a person must be involved in the workforce in covered employment or self-employment. He or she must earn a minimum number of credits in order to be eligible for any benefits. The actual amount of the determined benefit will depend on eligibility as well as how much the worker has earned (see below).

### *Credits or Quarters of Coverage*

Before 1978, employers reported wages every three months, called "quarters of coverage." A worker was credited with a quarter of coverage if he or she earned at least $50 in a quarter. Since 1978, earnings are reported yearly and credits are based on how much is earned during the year, up to a maximum of four credits for the year, regardless of when one works during the year. Each year, the amount it takes to earn a credit changes. For example, in 1995, one credit was earned for each $630 of covered annual earnings.

Generally, 40 credits (equivalent to ten years of work) are necessary to qualify for retirement benefits. (Younger people need fewer credits for disability or for their survivors if they should die.)

### *Calculation of Social Security Benefits*

A worker's Social Security benefit amount is based on his or her average covered earnings computed over a period of time equal to the number of years he or she could have reasonably been expected to work. Social Security benefits are not based on one's direct payroll contributions, but on earnings upon which taxes were paid.

Two calculations are done to determine a retiree's Social Security benefit. The first is a measure of the individual's average monthly earnings, and is calculated from the earnings record. This amount is then indexed to reflect the change in average wages that has occurred and is referred to as the AIME* (Average Indexed Monthly Earnings) calculation.

Next, using the AIME calculation, the worker's primary insurance amount (PIA) is determined. The PIA is the basis on which all Social Security benefits are made. For persons first eligible in 1995 the PIA formula is:

90 percent of the first $426 of AIME plus
32 percent of AIME between $426–$2,567, plus
15 percent of AIME above $2,567

(The dollar amounts in the formula are called "bend points" and are changed annually to reflect growth in wages. The percentages represent "replacement rates" and are formula constants.)

The PIA is the monthly benefit paid to a worker retiring at "normal retirement age," which is currently 65 years of age (see below). At 65, a person is eligible to collect full benefits. If one retires earlier, the PIA is reduced; and if a worker retires at a later age, the PIA is increased.

### *Eligibility Age*

The "normal retirement age" (i.e., the age of eligibility for full retirement benefits) will be increased

*Benefit calculations using the AIME formula commenced in 1979. For persons who became eligible before 1979, the actual amount of covered earnings (AME) is used in benefit determinations.

gradually from 65 to 67 beginning with workers who reach age 62 in the year 2000. Benefits will continue to be made available to those who retire at age 62, but the reduction in benefits will be greater. Currently, someone who retires at age 62 receives 80 percent of the full benefit amount, and a spouse who begins to receive benefits at age 62 receives 75 percent of the full benefit that would be available at age 65.

### *COLAs*

In general, after a person's initial Social Security benefit has been determined for the first year of eligibility (when he reaches age 62, becomes disabled, or dies) the amount is automatically increased each December to reflect increases in the Consumer Price Index (CPI). This is referred to as Cost-of-Living Adjustments, or COLAs.

### *Spousal/Family Benefits*

A person who is eligible for a benefit based on his or her own earnings and also for a benefit as an eligible family member (usually wife) or survivor (usually widow) will receive the full amount of his or her own benefit plus an amount equal to any excess of the other benefit—essentially the larger of the two.

### *Adjustments and Delayed Retirement Credit*

The benefit may also be recalculated if, after retirement, the worker has additional earnings that result in a higher PIA. And a worker who delays retirement past the normal retirement age of 65 has his or her benefits increased based on delayed retirement credit. The credit is currently being raised every other year. The credit is 5 percent of the PIA per year for workers who become 62 in 1993–94, and will increase to 5.5 percent of the PIA for workers who attain age 62 in 1995–96, and so on until it reaches 8 percent of the PIA per year for workers who reach age 62 in the year 2005 or later.

## *Reduction of Benefits*

If a beneficiary works, there are caps on how much a retiree can earn before Social Security benefits will be reduced. In 1995, beneficiaries age 65–69 may earn up to $11,280 and those under 65 may earn up to $8,160. Beneficiaries under age 65 have their benefits reduced $1 for each $2 in earnings over the annual exempt amount. Workers over age 65 reduce their benefit by $1 for every $3 earned, and persons aged 70 or older may earn any amount without a benefit reduction.

## *Taxation of Benefits**

***Tier 1*** Currently, a portion of Social Security benefits is included in gross income. Following 1983, benefits were to be included in gross income for beneficiaries whose provisional income exceeded $25,000 for unmarried and $32,000 for married couples

*These regulations apply to railroad retirement as well as Social Security beneficiaries.

filing jointly. Provisional income was defined as the sum of adjusted gross income (before Social Security benefits are considered) plus certain nontaxable income (such as tax-exempt interest income) and one half of Social Security benefits. If provisional income exceeds the base amount, individuals are required to include as part of gross income for tax purposes half of the difference between provisional income and the base amount, whichever is less.

***Tier 2*** In 1993, the taxation of benefits was increased to 85 percent for a second tier of base amounts—$34,000 for unmarried and $44,000 for married couples filing jointly. Thus, beneficiaries who earn up to these new amounts are still required to pay income taxes under the 1983 Tier 1 rules. Retirees whose incomes exceed these amounts must now include as part of gross income the lesser of 85 percent of their Social Security Tier 1 benefits or $4,500 for unmarried or $6,000 for married couples filing jointly, plus 85 percent of the excess of their provisional incomes over the Tier 2 amount.

### *Other Highlights*

- The SSA program was enacted in 1935, and celebrated its sixtieth anniversary on August 14, 1995.
- The SSA became an independent agency on March 31, 1995.
- Social Security is available to clients on the Internet (via FedWorld). One may request on-line estimate benefit calculations, read informational documents, and apply for a Social Security card.

- It is advisable to check one's Social Security account from time to time, to assure the accuracy of income reporting and to confirm that the requisite number of quarters have been posted on one's account. This can be done free by calling 1–800–772–1213 and requesting "Earnings Estimate Statement" SSA form #7004.

## MEDICARE/MEDICAID

Medicare, the health insurance program primarily intended for the elderly (and disabled), and the Medicaid program, designed to cover indigent populations, were both established by Congress in 1965. At the time, they were included in the Social Security Administration, under the Department of Health, Education, and Welfare (HEW). In 1977, Congress created the Health Care Financing Administration (HCFA), which now administers the Medicare and Medicaid programs, under the Department of Health and Human Services (HHS).

### *Medicare*

The Social Security Amendments of 1965 established two separate but related health insurance plans for persons 65 or older: the mandatory Hospital Insurance (HI) plan, known as Medicare Part A, and a voluntary program of Supplemental Medical Insurance (SMI), known as Part B.

## *Hospital Insurance (HI) Part A*

As with Social Security, mandatory contributions to HI are made on taxable earnings. The 1994 rate was 1.45 percent each for employers and employees, and 2.9 percent for self-employed workers. In 1994, the ceiling for taxable annual earnings was eliminated, so HI taxes apply to earnings in all covered employment.

Persons eligible for Social Security (or railroad retirement) benefits are eligible for premium-free HI benefits when they reach age 65. Also, HI protection is provided to disabled beneficiaries (not their dependents) who have been entitled to Social Security or railroad retirement benefits for 24 months, and to insured workers (and their spouses and children) with end-stage renal disease who require dialysis or a kidney transplant.

In addition, most persons aged 65 or older and otherwise ineligible for HI may voluntarily enroll and pay a monthly HI premium if also enrolled for SMI.

## *Benefits*

The following four types of medically necessary care are covered by Medicare Part A:

- Inpatient hospital care
- Inpatient care in a skilled nursing facility (SNF) following a hospital stay
- Home health care
- Hospice care

## *Inpatient hospital care*

Once a patient has paid the inpatient hospital deductible ($716 in 1995) he or she will be covered for all remaining costs of covered hospital services for the first 60 days. After that until day 90, the patient pays a daily coinsurance charge of one quarter the inpatient hospital deductible (in 1995, $179 per day). Medicare pays nothing after day 90, unless the beneficiary chooses to tap into his or her 60-day lifetime reserve.*

Covered services include routine hospital services: semiprivate room, operating room, laboratory and X-rays, drugs and biologicals, nursing services (not private duty), therapy services. Also covered is inpatient TB and psychiatric hospital care, with a lifetime limit of 190 days for the latter.

## *Post-Hospital Care: SNF*

Following a hospitalization of at least 3 days, a patient may be released to a skilled nursing facility (SNF) if daily skilled nursing or rehabilitation, but not hospital care, is required. The first 20 days of SNF are fully covered, but for days 21–100, a copay ($89.90 in 1995) is required. After the 100 days, Medicare contributes nothing to SNF care.

* Each Medicare beneficiary is entitled to a 60-day lifetime reserve that may be used when covered days are exhausted, and this may be used only once in one's lifetime. The coinsurance each day is one half the inpatient deductible (in 1995 it was $358 per day).

## *Home Health Care*

Unlimited home visits are covered if the patient is homebound and a physician determines that he or she needs intermittent* skilled nursing care and/or physical or speech therapy.

Durable medical equipment is subject to 20 percent coinsurance. Home health care has no deductible and no coinsurance.

## *Hospice Care*

Beneficiaries who are certified as terminally ill are covered for two 90-day periods, then a 30-day period, and then a subsequent extension of unlimited duration. Coverage includes physician and nursing care, medical appliances and supplies, drugs for symptom relief, short-term inpatient care, counseling, therapies, and home health and homemaker assistance. The Part A and B deductibles do not apply to hospice benefit services.

## *Supplemental Medical Insurance (SMI) Part B*

An individual is eligible for SMI on a voluntary basis by paying a monthly premium if he or she is:

- Entitled to premium-free hospital insurance protection

*Intermittent is defined as no more than four days per week; daily skilled nursing visits up to eight hours per day for up to three weeks.

- Age 65 or older, a resident of the United States, and either a citizen of the United States or a legal alien admitted for permanent residence

Cost-sharing contributions are required, which include:

- One annual deductible (currently $100)
- Monthly premiums ($46.10 in 1995—deducted from Social Security benefit)
- Coinsurance payments for Part B services (20 percent allowable charges)
- Charges above the Medicare allowed charge (not on assignment)
- Payment for any uncovered Medicare services

It is important to note that there is no ceiling on out-of-pocket expenses that can be incurred under Medicare. Thus, a long-term hospitalization can use up all of a patient's financial resources before Medicaid eligibility begins.

The scope of covered services and supplies in the SMI program include:

- Physician and surgeon fees; some covered services by chiropractors, podiatrists, dentists, and optometrists (but not routine care)
- The following non–medical doctor approved practitioners and services:
    1. certified registered nurse anesthetists
    2. clinical psychologists

3. clinical social workers (other than in skilled nursing facility)
4. physician assistants
5. nurse practitioners and clinical nurse specialists

- Services in an emergency room, outpatient clinic, same-day surgery
- Laboratory tests, X-rays and other radiology services billed by hospital, approved independent lab services, portable X-ray services, Pap screen, and mammography
- Mental health care in partial-hospitalization psychiatric program, if medical doctor certifies inpatient treatment would be otherwise required
- Ambulatory surgical center services
- Physical and occupational therapy, speech pathology, skilled nursing facility, participating home health agency, rehabilitation agency
- Comprehensive outpatient rehabilitation, nonhospital treatment of mental illness, and partial hospitalization for mental health treatments
- Rural health clinic services, ambulance transportation under certain conditions
- Radiation therapy, renal dialysis and transplants, heart and liver transplants under certain conditions
- Approved durable medical equipment for home use, (e.g. oxygen equipment, wheelchairs, prosthetic devices)
- Drugs and biologicals that cannot be self-administered, blood and blood component transfusions, immunosuppressive drugs, antigens, epogen

for anemia related to chronic kidney failure or for HIV-positive beneficiaries

## *Coordinated Care Plans—HMOs*

Some health maintenance organizations (HMOs) contract with Medicare and arrange for all covered services. These plans usually charge fixed monthly premiums and small copayments. They may also offer benefits not covered by Medicare, such as preventive care, dental care, hearing aids, and eyeglasses. Also, the costs to the beneficiary may be less than the regular Medicare deductibles and coinsurance charges.

***Medigap Insurance*** Private insurance that pays the health care service charges not covered by Medicare Part A or B. *Medigap policies are not part of Medicare.* In 1990, Congress directed that standards be set for Medigap policies. It required open enrollment, and said that a policy could not be canceled or renewal refused based on the health status of the policyholder. Also, it standardized the ten Medigap policies that could be sold, which must cover specific expenses not fully covered by Medicare. Plan "A" is the most basic policy and plan "J" the most comprehensive. To ease comparison among plans and premiums for the consumer, standard formats, language, and description of benefits must be used.

## MEDICAID

Medicaid is a federal-state* matching entitlement program, established in 1965 under Title XIX of the Social Security Act. It is primarily intended to offer medical assistance for individuals and families of low incomes and resources.

Medicaid differs from Medicare in two significant ways:

- Medicaid is a means-tested program, while Medicare is not.
- While benefits for Medicare are established on a federal level and are fairly uniform throughout the country, Medicaid is administered by the states and varies considerably. So, within broad national guidelines, each state:
    1. sets its own eligibility standards.
    2. determines the range and scope of covered services.
    3. establishes rates of payment to providers.
    4. handles the administration of the program.

### *Eligibility*

The following are mandatory Medicaid eligibility groups:

*The state of Arizona does not operate a traditional Medicaid program. In 1982, it received a demonstration waiver to operate a federally assisted medical assistance program for low-income residents.

- Recipients of Aid to Families with Dependent Children (AFDC)
- Recipients of Supplemental Security Income (SSI), or aged, blind, or disabled persons in a state with more restrictive requirements
- Children under age six who meet the state's AFDC financial requirements or whose family income is equal to or at 133 percent of the federal poverty level
- Recipients of adoption assistance/foster care under Title IV-E of Social Security Act
- Pregnant women whose family income is below 133 percent of federal poverty level (services limited to pregnancy, delivery, postpartum care)
- Special protected groups whose status for cash assistance changes but are granted a temporary extension of Medicaid coverage

These groups are sometimes referred to as "categorically needy" groups.

In addition, states have the option to provide Medicaid coverage to other groups for which they will receive federal matching funds. These include expanded populations of "categorically needy" as well as groups known as "medically needy." (Often the distinction between these two groups is difficult to make.)

The Medicare Catastrophic Care Act (MCCA) of 1988 made significant changes that impacted Medicaid. Although MCCA was repealed the following year, many of the Medicaid changes remained in effect. Among these were changes that accelerated Medicaid eligibility for some nursing home patients by shielding more income and assets for the institutionalized person's spouse living at home.

## *Range of Services for Medicaid*

Under Title XIX, certain basic services must be offered in order for states to receive federal matching funds. These include:

- Inpatient hospital services
- Outpatient hospital services
- Physician services
- Prenatal care
- Nursing facility services for persons 21 and older
- Home health care for persons eligible for skilled nursing services
- Family planning services and supplies
- Laboratory and X-ray services
- Rural health clinics
- Pediatric and family nurse practitioner services
- Nurse midwife services
- Certain federally funded qualified ambulatory and health center services
- Early and periodic screening, diagnosis, and treatment (EPSDT) for children under 21

Also, optional services may be covered, and commonly include:

- Clinic services
- Nursing facilities for the aged and disabled
- Intermediate care facilities for the mentally retarded
- Optometrist services and eyeglasses
- Prescription drugs

- Prosthetic devices
- Dental services

With some exceptions, a state must allow Medicaid recipients freedom of choice among participating health providers. States may provide and pay for Medicaid services through various prepayment arrangements, such as HMOs.

### *Medicare-Medicaid Relationship*

Some aged (or disabled) persons are covered under both Medicaid and Medicare. The state Medicaid agency may pay SMI premiums for Medicaid recipients who are entitled to Medicare. Also, for Medicare recipients who are also fully eligible for Medicaid, Medicare coverage is supplemented by health care services that are available under the state's Medicaid program, but not covered under Medicare (e.g., prescriptions, prosthetic devices, nursing facility care beyond the 100-day Medicare limit).

There are also some individuals who are not fully eligible for Medicaid but who receive some assistance through the state's Medicaid program for part or all of the person's Medicare premiums and copays:

- Qualified disabled and working individuals (QDWIDs). Disabled persons who lost Medicare benefits because they returned to work can purchase Medicare Parts A and B. However, the Part A premium must be paid by the state Medicaid program for disabled workers with incomes below 200 percent of the federal poverty level; they are not required to pay for the Part B premiums for these persons.

- Qualified Medicare Beneficiaries (QMBs)
- Specified Low-Income Medicare Beneficiaries (SLMBs)

QMBs have resources at or below two times the standard allowed under the SSI program and with incomes below the federal poverty guidelines. They are eligible for state payment of all premiums and cost-sharing expenses for Parts A and B of Medicare.

For SLMBs, with slightly higher incomes than QMBs (less than 120 percent of federal poverty guidelines in 1995), the state is required to pay the Part B premiums. Also, payments for Medicare-covered services are paid by Medicare first—Medicaid is always the payer of last resort.

## *Transfer of Assets—OBRA 1993**

This provision delays Medicaid eligibility for institutionalized persons (or their spouses) receiving nursing home care (or the equivalent) and to noninstitutionalized persons receiving alternative care (home or community-based) who dispose of their assets for less than fair market value on or after a specific "look-back" date (36 months prior to either the date of benefits application, or the date beginning institutional care, whichever is later). Penalties are not

*OBRA 1993 is the Omnibus Budget Reconciliation Act of 1993.

applied to transfers to spouses or, under certain conditions, to minors or disabled children.

### *Medicaid Estate Recoveries—OBRA 1993*

States are required to recover from the estates of Medicaid recipients the costs of nursing facility and other long-term care services furnished to them. Procedures are established for waivers in cases of hardship.

# Note on Sources

The most important printed sources are set out below, supplemented by some specific comments on sources for individual chapters.

Aaron, Henry J. "Sowing the Seeds of Reform in 1994." *Health Affairs*, Spring 1994.

———. "Thinking Straight About Medical Costs." *Health Affairs*, Winter 1994.

———. *Serious and Unstable Condition: Financing America's Health Care.* Washington, D.C.: Brookings, 1991.

Aaron, Henry J., and Barry P. Bosworth. "Economic Issues in Reform of Health Care Financing." *Brookings Papers on Economic Activity*. Washington, D.C.: Brookings, 1994.

Aaron, Henry J., Barry P. Bosworth, and Gary Burtless. *Can America Afford to Grow Old? Paying for Social Security*. Washington, D.C.: Brookings, 1989.

Agency for Health Care Policy and Research. *Nursing Home Use and Costs: Lifetime Estimates and the Effect of Financing Strategies*. Washington, D.C.: U.S. Government Printing Office, 1993.

———. *Research Summaries: Long-Term Care Studies.* Washington, D.C.: U.S. Government Printing Office, 1993.

American Association of Retired Persons. *Annual Reports.*

———. "AARP Focus on Social Security." *Modern Maturity*, June/July 1995.

———. *Entitlements and the Federal Budget Deficit: Setting the Record Straight.* Washington, D.C.: AARP, 1994, 1995.

———. *Aging Baby Boomers: How Secure Is Their Economic Future?* Washington, D.C.: AARP, 1994.

———. *Toward a Just and Caring Society: The AARP Public Policy Agenda, 1995.* Washington, D.C.: AARP, 1995.

———. "Issue Brief, Old Age Insurance: Who Gets What for Their Money." October 1992.

Baumol, William J. "Containing Medical Costs: Why Price Controls Won't Work." *The Public Interest,* Fall 1988.

Baumol, William J., Sue Anne Batey, and Edward N. Wolff. *Productivity and American Leadership: The Long View.* Cambridge, Mass.: MIT Press, 1989.

Bipartisan Commission on Entitlement and Tax Reform. *Final Report to the President.* Washington, D.C.: U.S. Government Printing Office, 1995.

Board of Trustees, Federal Hospital Insurance Trust Fund. *1995 Annual Report.* Washington, D.C.: U.S. Government Printing Office, 1995.

Board of Trustees, Federal Old-Age and Survivors Insurance and Disability Insurance Trust Funds. *1995 Annual Report.* Washington, D.C.: U.S. Government Printing Office, 1995.

Board of Trustees, Federal Supplementary Medical Insurance Trust Fund. *1995 Annual Report.* Washington, D.C.: U.S. Government Printing Office, 1995.

Cox, Hank. "Age Before Beauty: American Association of Retired Persons." *Regardie's*, January 1991.

DYG, Inc. "Social Security and Medicare Anniversary Research: A Study of Public Attitudes and Values." New York, 1995.

Emanuel, Ezekiel, and Linda L. Emanuel. "The Economics of Dying—The Illusion of Cost Savings at the End of Life." *New England Journal of Medicine*, February 24, 1994.

Glaser, William A. "The Competition Vogue and Its Outcomes." *The Lancet*, March 27, 1993.

Health Care Financing Administration. "Personal Health Care Expenditures: 1992 Highlights." *Health Care Financing Review*, 1995 Statistical Supplement.

House Republican Conference, Medicare Communications Group. "Everything You Ever Wanted to Know About Communicating Medicare," June 8, 1995.

Hudson, Terese. "Medicaid: Will the Public Program Neglect the Poor to Pay for the Elderly?" *Hospital and Health Networks*, May 1995.

Keeler, Emmett B., et al. *The Demand for Episodes of Medical Treatment in the Health Insurance Experiment.* Santa Monica, Calif.: Rand, 1988.

Levit, Katherine R., et al. "National Health Spending Trends, 1960–1993." *Health Affairs*, Winter 1994.

Longman, Phillip. "Catastrophic Follies: The Old Folks Outfox Themselves: Medicare Catastrophic Coverage Act." *The New Republic*, August 21, 1989.

Marmor, Theodore R., and Jerry Mashaw. "Retire the Insolvency Myth." *Los Angeles Times*, July 30, 1995.

National Institutes of Health and National Institute on Aging. *Progress Report on Alzheimer's Disease, 1994.* Washington, D.C.: U.S. Government Printing Office, 1994.

Peterson, Peter G. *Facing Up: Paying Our Nation's Debt and Saving Our Children's Future.* New York: Simon and Schuster, 1994.

Pilote, L., et al. "Differences in the Treatment of Myocardial Infarction in the United States and Canada: A Comparison of Two University Hospitals." *Archives of Internal Medicine*, May 23, 1994.

Rauch, Jonathan. *Demosclerosis: The Silent Killer of American Government.* New York: Times Books, 1994.

Relman, Arnold S. "The New Medical-Industrial Complex." *New England Journal of Medicine*, October 23, 1980.

Rouleau, J. L., et al. "A Comparison of Management Patterns After Acute Myocardial Infarction in Canada and the United States." *New England Journal of Medicine*, March 18, 1993.

Schwarz, William B, and Daniel N. Mendelsen. "Eliminating Waste and Inefficiency Can Do Little to Contain Costs." *Health Affairs*, Spring, 1994.

Social Security Administration, Office of the Actuary. *History of the Provisions of Old-Age, Survivors, Disability, and Health Insurance: 1935–1993.* Washington, D.C.: U.S. Government Printing Office, 1994.

Steurele, Eugene C., and Jon M. Bakija. *Retooling Social Security for the Twenty-First Century: Right and*

*Wrong Approaches to Reform*. Washington, D.C.: The Urban Institute, 1994.

Stockman, David A. *The Triumph of Politics: Why the Reagan Revolution Failed*. New York: Harper and Row, 1986.

Street, Debra. "Maintaining the Status Quo: The Impact of Old-Age Interest Groups on the Medicare Catastrophic Coverage Act of 1988." *Social Problems*, November 1993.

U.S. General Accounting Office. *Long-Term Care: Current Issues and Future Directions*. Washington, D.C.: U.S. Government Printing Office, 1995.

U.S. House of Representatives, Ways and Means Committee. *Green Book of Entitlement Programs*. Washington, D.C.: U.S. Government Printing Office, 1994.

U.S. Senate, Special Committee on Aging. *Aging America: Trends and Projections*. Washington, D.C.: U.S. Government Printing Office, 1991.

Williamson, Jeffrey G. "Productivity and American Leadership: A Review Article." *Journal of Economic Literature*, March 1991.

## OTHER SOURCES

Except as the text or context makes clear, or as noted below, direct quotations are from interviews. For the early years of AARP, in addition to publicly available material from the financial and other press, and historical material published by AARP, I had the use of an extensive file of primary sources compiled by Andy Rooney and his staff at CBS. The history of the legislative struggles in chapter 6 relies heavily on an interview narrative by Martin Corry, which tracked well with the detailed accounts in the *Congressional Quarterly* and that of the Stockman book. I used the *CQ* as the primary chronological reference. Unless otherwise indicated, quotes in chapter 6 are from the accounts in *CQ*.

# Index

## About the Author

Charles R. Morris writes on politics, business, and economics for *The Atlantic Monthly*, *The New York Times Magazine*, the *Los Angeles Times*, and many other publications. This is his sixth book.